James McLeskey

Nancy L. Waldron

Inclusive Schools in Action

Making Differences Ordinary

Association for Supervision and Curriculum Development Alexandria, Virginia USA

Association for Supervision and Curriculum Development
1703 N. Beauregard St. • Alexandria, VA 22311-1714 USA
Telephone: 1-800-933-2723 or 703-578-9600 • Fax: 703-575-5400
Web site: http://www.ascd.org • E-mail: member@ascd.org

Michelle Terry, *Deputy Executive Director, Program Development*
Nancy Modrak, *Director of Publishing*
John O'Neil, *Director of Acquisitions*
Robert W. Cole, *Development Editor*
Julie Houtz, *Managing Editor of Books*
Jo Ann Irick Jones, *Senior Associate Editor*
Darcie Russell, *Project Manager*
EEI Communications, *Copy Editor*
Bob Land, *Proofreader*
Ernesto Yermoli, *Project Assistant*
Gary Bloom, *Director, Design and Production Services*
Georgia McDonald, *Senior Designer*
Dina Murray Seamon, *Production Coordinator*
Cindy Stock, *Desktop Publisher*
Coughlin Indexing Services, Inc., *Indexer*

Printed in the United States of America.

ASCD Product No. 100210   s12/00
ASCD member price: $19.95 nonmember price: $23.95

Library of Congress Cataloging-in-Publication Data
McLeskey, James, 1949–
    Inclusive schools in action : making differences ordinary / James McLeskey and Nancy L. Waldron.
        p. cm.
Includes bibliographical references (p.) and index.
    ISBN 0-87120-389-8 (alk. paper)
    1. Inclusive education—United States. I. Waldron, Nancy L. II. Title.
    LC1201 .M39 2000
    371.9'046—dc21   00-011251

06 05 04 03 02 01 00   10 9 8 7 6 5 4 3 2 1

Inclusive Schools in Action: Making Differences Ordinary

Acknowledgments

For the past 12 years, we have worked with scores of administrators and teachers who have shared their ideas and passions with us regarding inclusive schools. Much of what we have to say in this book comes from what we've learned from these collaborative endeavors. In particular, we thank the teachers and administrators from the Monroe County Community School Corporation (Bloomington, Indiana), Bartholomew Consolidated School Corporation (Columbus, Indiana), and Greater Clark County Schools (Jeffersonville, Indiana). These educators opened the doors of their schools and classrooms to us, shared many great ideas, and helped us understand the benefits and challenges of developing inclusive programs. Three educators in these settings were longtime collaborators: Sandi Cole, Barbara Horvath, and Ann Schnepf. We would like to thank them for their support and insights.

Introduction

Inclusion and School Change

For the last 30 years (Cegelka & Tyler, 1970; Dunn, 1968; Goldstein, Moss, & Jordan, 1965), educators have criticized separate classes for most students with disabilities, recommending that they be educated in general education classrooms with age-appropriate peers for much of the school day. While receiving strong support in the professional literature, in practice this movement—variously known as mainstreaming, the regular education initiative, integration, and, most recently, inclusion—has met with mixed success. For example, many of the programs developed during the mainstreaming movement of the 1970s and 1980s were add-on programs that were attached to ongoing school activities without questioning or changing the curriculum and instructional practices in general education classrooms. Consider the following example:

EXAMPLE

I was teaching 45 students who were labeled mildly and moderately retarded in a Quonset hut behind a vocational high school. Two other certified teachers and a paraprofessional worked with me to teach these students. Several of the students were being mainstreamed into vocational classes, including auto mechanics, textiles, and brick masonry, as well as special area classes (art, music, and physical education). Our students were also involved in extracurricular

—continued—

1

EXAMPLE

—continued—

activities, including varsity basketball and football, and two or three, at any point in time, were involved in work-study programs. We felt that we were making much progress toward educating our students in settings with typical peers, both in school and in the community, although we were facing considerable opposition in this endeavor from teachers and members of the community.

In the latter part of the second semester, an assistant superintendent visited my classroom and said he wanted to discuss a new movement he had heard and read about, suggesting that the students in my class should be educated with typical peers. When I had a break, we talked about his concerns, which addressed, among other things, the overrepresentation of African American students and students from low-income homes in classes such as mine (my class was an extremely good example of this phenomenon) and the contention that segregated special education classes were not in the best interest of students with mild/moderate mental retardation. He went on to comment that it was clear to him that these students would learn best with the positive models and high expectations of the general education classroom. I soon realized that the assistant superintendent was determined to correct the error of our ways and mainstream the students I was teaching. He noted that there was not space for a classroom in the vocational high school for us (thus, the Quonset hut) and that we would have to relocate to another high school in the city. The other high school was very academically oriented, most students went on to college, and there were no vocational programs. I suggested that perhaps the curriculum of the vocational high school was more appropriate for my students, because it was highly unlikely that any of them would go to college. The assistant superintendent brushed off my comment and was clearly not convinced by my reasoning.

I then asked if the teachers in the other high school had been contacted regarding this proposed change, because they should be

—continued—

—continued—

EXAMPLE

involved in this decision and would be integral to the success of the proposed program. The assistant superintendent said that he had just come up with the idea and had not yet talked with the teachers in the other high school. He added that he didn't plan on telling the teachers because he didn't want them to have low expectations for these students. Thus, he wanted to place (dump) the students in general education classes at the beginning of the next school year and place me in a resource class to provide the teachers and students with needed support. As my curiosity rose further, I asked about the two other teachers and the paraprofessional who currently were teaching these students. He said that with this new program, classroom teachers would provide much support for these students; thus, fewer teachers would be needed. He then stated that the paraprofessional and I should be able to provide high-quality services for these students.

I suggested that this change in services was not in the best interest of the students and said that I would quit if this change were made (I was young and naive—stupid—and felt that I mattered). The assistant superintendent readily accepted my resignation and hired a new teacher to take on this new role. While teaching the following year in a nearby school, I followed the progress of the 30 students who went from my class to the new high school program (several students graduated, and a few dropped out over the summer because of a variety of issues, including pregnancy and imprisonment). By the end of the first semester, 29 of the 30 students who had moved to the new school had dropped out. The only student who remained was a very large, jovial, good-natured young man who got along with everyone and was frequently found walking the halls delivering notes and carrying lunch money to the principal's office.

Unfortunately, even with the advent of the school reform and inclusion movements in the late 1980s and early 1990s (Sailor, 1991; McLeskey, Skiba, & Wilcox, 1990; Will, 1986), there continue to be all too many examples of inclusion programs using this add-on approach that are mandated by misguided "leaders" in a school system (for example, see Baines, Baines, & Masterson, 1994; Fox & Ysseldyke, 1997; Shanker, 1994/1995). Obviously, such an approach is not in the best interest of students with disabilities or their teachers. Would the students in the preceding example have been better off remaining in the Quonset hut rather than being mainstreamed? Our answer is unequivocally, yes! This add-on program mandated change, excluded teachers from planning and decision making, reduced resources as the program was implemented, dumped students with disabilities into general education classrooms with no support, failed to change the general education classrooms so that students with disabilities could be better accommodated, and diminished the quality of the education that was being provided to all students. In a nutshell, *no one* benefited from the implementation of this mainstreaming program.

In contrast to this high school, there are well-documented examples of practices that lead to successful school change, as well as successful inclusion of students with disabilities into general education classrooms. Successful schools involve teachers in planning and decision making, provide support for students with disabilities in general education classrooms, and achieve positive academic and social outcomes for students with and without disabilities. These successful practices also take much time and planning to implement and cannot be mandated. Consider the following example (Cole & McLeskey, 1997):

EXAMPLE

Planning for inclusion at "Roosevelt High School" began two years before the program was implemented. The initial discussions began among a group of teachers who realized that although Roosevelt had a highly successful program for students with more substantial needs (these students were educated with age-appropriate peers in general education classrooms, gained vocational skills through a work-study program, and often left school with paid employment), the program

—continued—

EXAMPLE

—continued—

for students with mild disabilities was much less successful. These students took most of their courses in core content areas in special classes that were taught by special education teachers and which included only other students with disabilities. The teachers also concluded that the academic expectations for these students were very low and that most of them left school with few of the skills required for successful employment in the community. After examining the special education program for students with mild disabilities and visiting other high school programs, the teachers and administration decided that their program was in need of much improvement.

Based on the information these teachers collected and initial discussions, a team of teachers began meeting to develop a plan for improving the educational program for students with mild disabilities. This group drafted a written proposal that was presented to the Roosevelt faculty. As part of this proposal, the team of teachers identified two sections in which the new program would be piloted: a 9th grade general math class and an 11th grade English class. The proposal was built upon the premise that general and special education teachers would work as partners and transform the curriculum and instruction of the general education classroom so that the needs of all students could be better addressed. The teachers and administration at Roosevelt gave this proposal their strong support.

Over the following summer, the four teachers who volunteered to team in the English and math classes were provided support to plan the curriculum and instruction they would use in their classrooms. The following fall, two years after planning began, the first inclusion classes began at Roosevelt High School. These classes were highly successful. The planning team continued to meet, and other teachers volunteered to participate in the inclusion program in subsequent years. Seven years later, the number of self-contained classes for students with mild disabilities at Roosevelt had been reduced from 21 to 3, and the number of sections that were collaboratively taught was extended to all curricular content areas and grade levels.

Overview of the Book

From these examples and others like them, we have learned many important lessons about how successful inclusive school programs are developed and why some are unsuccessful. The following chapters address many of these lessons.

Over the past decade we have worked with numerous schools across a range of school districts as they have developed, implemented, and improved inclusive programs. These schools were largely in a Midwestern state and represent all grade levels and a range of community settings that were urban, suburban, and rural. Our activities with these schools have included presenting workshops on a variety of topics related to inclusion, conducting evaluations of inclusive programs in local school districts, and assisting school-based planning teams.

Participating on planning teams provided us the opportunity to work with teachers and administrators over a six-month to two-year period as they grappled with the issues of understanding inclusion, developing a vision and a plan for their own school, and implementing and revising their inclusive programs. Through this process we have found ourselves assuming various roles with planning teams, based on their individual school needs and interests. These roles have included serving as consultants, researchers, collaborators, advocates, listeners, change agents, provocateurs, and even cheerleaders.

The examples we present throughout the book are drawn from situations we have observed in schools and classrooms, and the words of the teachers and administrators as conveyed during team planning meetings, faculty meetings, and interviews with educators involved in inclusive schools. The names of students, educators, and schools used are pseudonyms. These elementary, middle, and high school educators have taught us much of what we know and understand about inclusive schools. Through their words and actions we hope to share this understanding with other educators who continue the important work of developing and improving inclusive schools for all students.

We begin in Chapter 1 with a review of issues regarding school change and inclusion. Included are topics such as the need to change the entire school and not just special education as inclusive programs are developed, the ripple (systemic) effect of any change in a school, the need to empower teachers and administrators to manage their own change, the need to tailor changes to the unique needs of the local school, and the warning to expect resistance when any major change is undertaken. This chapter provides a critical foundation for the remainder of the book, as we have found that if stakeholders in schools are to successfully achieve school change, they need to know a great deal about how and why schools change.

In Chapter 2, we address the need for leadership in changing schools and developing inclusive programs. While it is axiomatic to say that the principal is the key leader in any school change effort, it is important to understand that leadership takes many forms and must come from many individuals if school change is to be successful.

Chapter 3 addresses organizational and systemic issues that must be addressed for a school to develop a successful inclusive program. Topics addressed include the need for adequate time to plan and implement the program, for staff development, for balance between natural proportions and intensity of services, and for examining how the school day is organized. Other issues discussed include the unique role of the special education teacher and how to maintain inclusive programs.

In Chapter 4, we examine teacher beliefs, attitudes, and under-standing regarding inclusion, as well as methods to examine and change these teacher concepts as inclusive programs are developed. We take the perspective that inclusive schools will be successful only if they have the support of the teachers who are responsible for implementing the programs, and that teachers must understand why inclusion is important and must believe that they can develop and implement an effective program.

Chapter 5 addresses the logistics that must be considered when developing and implementing inclusive classrooms. Some of the topics addressed are including all students in the learning and social community of the classroom, making difference ordinary in the general education classroom, establishing student supports that are natural and unobtrusive, and making the "rhythm of the day" for students with disabilities as typical as possible.

Chapter 6 reviews changes that can be made in classrooms to better meet the wide range of student *academic* needs, ensuring that all students become part of the academic community of the classroom. Chapter 7 looks at changes to make in the general education classroom to better meet the *social* needs of students, thus ensuring that all students are members of the social community of the classroom. (The resource guide provided in the appendix includes books, chapters, articles, and materials that may be used to address the academic and social needs of all students in general education classrooms.)

Chapter 8 begins by addressing issues that are specific to secondary schools and then looks at four examples of changes that have been made in secondary schools as they have developed inclusive school programs. Topics addressed include changing the curriculum, altering the school day, developing teaching partnerships, and developing instructional communities to support inclusion.

Chapter 9 provides an example of a systematic approach that may be used to develop and implement an inclusive school program. Emphasis is also placed on tailoring the approach to school change to the specific needs of the local school. Also included is a series of activities we have used with school-based teams as they have worked toward developing inclusive schools.

Finally, Chapter 10 pulls together information from the preceding chapters into lessons learned as we have worked with schools to develop, implement, and maintain inclusive schools.

Issues Related to School Change and Inclusion

A s members of a school community consider the issue of inclusion, it is important for them to recognize that the development and implementation of such a program entails significant changes in the entire school. Inclusion cannot and should not be limited to students with disabilities and their teachers. Schools are simply too complex and the various components of the school are too interrelated and interdependent for isolated changes to occur. The following sections provide a rationale for viewing inclusion not as simply a change in special education services but rather as an opportunity for school reform or renewal, that is, changing a school so that the needs of *all* students are better met. Initially discussed is a reality of school change that every teacher will readily recognize: that any change in a school has a ripple effect, influencing various other components of the school. Next is a discussion of the need to make substantive changes in the entire school as an inclusive program is developed. These changes cannot be simply added on to ongoing school practices. To achieve these changes, schools must be empowered to make the changes that stakeholders in the school community feel are needed to make the program successful. This is done by tailoring the necessary changes to the individual needs, strengths, and preferences of the school administration and faculty who will be implementing the program. Finally, the discussion turns to the need to expect resistance or at least serious questions about changes that are being proposed as the inclusive program is being developed and implemented.

The Ripple Effect of Change

Once one of the authors was working with a group of teachers and administrators as they were considering whether they would develop an inclusive school program. During a discussion early in this process, I stated bluntly that students were labeled with disabilities because they couldn't do exactly what everyone else could do in the area of their disability. Thus, if these students were going to be successfully included in general education classrooms, it was necessary that teacher expectations be changed for these students, and that the classroom curriculum, instruction, and grading be adapted. During the next break, a 3rd grade teacher from the school took me aside and adamantly stated that she could not make the changes in her classroom that were being suggested. As we began discussing her concerns, she asked a question: "Do you know who the biggest critic of a 3rd grade teacher is?" I didn't have an immediate response and said, "No." She immediately said, "A 4th grade teacher. You are asking me to send students to 4th grade with my 'stamp of approval' that they've sufficiently mastered the curriculum of 3rd grade, with good grades that indicate this has occurred. When the 4th grade teacher gets these students, she will know that this is not the case, and whom will she blame?" She went on to express her concern regarding the message this change would send to parents, other students in her classroom, and school board members.

This teacher's point is valid and extremely important to consider as inclusive school programs are being developed and implemented. Another way of thinking about this issue is that every change that occurs in a school has a ripple effect. If a single teacher in a classroom adapts the curriculum and has different expectations for a student, this act is influenced by the opinions and perspectives of the teacher at the next grade level, other students in the classroom, parents' views of grading, the principal's perspective on adaptations and student expectations, statewide testing programs, school

10

accreditation criteria, school board policies, and a plethora of other issues.

Sarason (1990) further illustrates this point as he reflects on the difficulty of school change. Sarason suggests an exercise in which participants imagine they have been empowered to make one, and only one, change in a school. The only restriction is that this change must not cost significantly more money than is currently being spent. As this single change is considered, it quickly becomes obvious that it is impossible to change only one thing within a school, because changes are "so embedded in a system of interacting parts that if [one thing] is changed, then changes elsewhere are likely to occur" (p. 16). This exercise illustrates the fact that schools and classrooms are complex systems that are influenced by and influence many factors both inside and outside the schools. This complexity led Sarason to state that schools could not be changed without considering the many systems that influence them. "I came to see what should have been obvious: the characteristics, traditions, and organizational dynamics of school systems were more or less lethal obstacles to achieving even modest, narrow goals" (p. 12).

Fullan and Miles (1992) address what it means to work systemically in a school to bring about change. They suggest that if school change is to be successful, it must "focus on the development and interrelationships of all the main *components* of the system simultaneously—curriculum, teaching and teacher development, community, student support systems, and so on" (p. 751). They go on to note that "reform must focus not just on structure, policy, and regulations but on deeper issues of the *culture* of the system" (p. 751).

Perhaps the most difficult aspect of systemic change is understanding and changing the culture of the school. As Sarason (1995) states, the culture of a school "refers to those aspects of the setting that are viewed by school personnel as 'givens' or essential features, which they would strenuously defend against elimination or marked change" (p. 71). These beliefs are often so much a part of a school setting that they are not given much thought. They are simply "the way things are." Practices that are widely held within a school must be identified and questioned if school change is to be successful. For example, should all students be expected to master the same curriculum at the same time? Should all students be expected to move through the curriculum at the same pace? Should students who are a certain age by a certain date be grouped into a classroom with other students of a similar age for the entire school day? Should all students be graded based on the same criteria? Should teachers close their classroom doors and work alone?

To state the patently obvious: Inclusion requires substantive change. Change that influences every aspect of a school. Change that alters the daily professional activities of teachers and administrators. Change that alters how students are taught, what they are taught, how they are grouped to receive instruction, and who delivers that instruction. Change that challenges traditional attitudes, beliefs, and understandings regarding students with disabilities and other students who do not "fit" into the typical classroom in a school.

To achieve the changes that are necessary, both general and special education teachers must be supportive of and involved in planning and implementing the inclusive school. Inclusion is not, and cannot be, just a "special education" issue; it requires changes in the professional practices of all teachers in a school. Indeed, as was recently demonstrated by Fox and Ysseldyke (1997), if an inclusive program is developed by special education teachers with little or no involvement of general education teachers, what is likely to result is a program that is tantamount to moving special education programs into general education classrooms but keeping them isolated from the "mainstream" of the classroom. Such a program is the epitome of what Fullan (1993) characterizes as superficial change, and it is sure to fail.

Transformation of School Practices

EXAMPLE

Ms. Austin had been a teacher in a separate special education class in an elementary school for several years. Her school developed an inclusive program, and she was assigned to work with three teachers at the primary level. All the students with disabilities who were identified in grades 1–3 were clustered into three classes, one

—continued—

EXAMPLE

—continued—

at each grade level, and Ms. Austin spent part of the school day with each of these teachers. One teacher, Ms. Patton, who taught 3rd grade, did not support inclusion and felt that she should not have to change her classroom routine because of "this new fad, inclusion." One of the authors observed Ms. Patton's class on a Thursday morning as the class began one hour of reading instruction. Ms. Austin entered the room at 9 a.m., and several children greeted her and gathered at a table at the back of the room. Ms. Patton continued her instruction of the large group of students, while Ms. Austin began small-group instruction with her group. Throughout reading instructional time, Ms. Austin and Ms. Patton did not interact, nor did the children who were in their respective groups. At the end of the reading session, Ms. Austin departed, and the students who had been in her reading group rejoined the other students for instruction.

Ms. Austin's experience provides an example of superficial change, an "add-on" program that is called "inclusion." This approach amounts to simply replicating special education services in the general education classroom, while keeping students with disabilities and their teacher substantially segregated from the learning community of the general education classroom. Our response to this type of "inclusion" program is "Why go to all the trouble to move the special education program intact from one location to another?" Indeed, a central goal of inclusion should be substantive change that transforms and improves education, not simply a change in location for currently existent special education services.

This approach to "inclusion" is reminiscent of the mainstreaming movement. Indeed, the implementation of mainstreaming programs over the past 30 years is a classic example of "add-on" programs of school change. When a student is mainstreamed, it is often assumed that the student will do the same work, behave the same way, and so forth, as other students in the class. The student is expected to adapt to the general education classroom, at times with the assistance of the special education teacher, who will record books, read tests to the student, and so forth. Throughout the mainstreaming movement, it has been taken for granted that the general education classroom will not change substantially (or at all, in many cases). The bottom line throughout the mainstreaming movement has been that *the student will adapt* and be ready to participate in the general education classroom, and *that the general education classroom will not change.* In contrast to this perspective, the inclusion movement assumes that *major changes will occur in the general education classroom,* ensuring that students with disabilities will "fit into" these classes. Thus, the general education classroom curriculum, instructional practices, organization, and so forth are changed to better meet the needs of the students, rather than expecting the students to adapt to the classroom. Given these criteria, Ms. Austin's experience is much more like mainstreaming than like inclusion.

In responding to a similar "add-on" type of inclusion program, Pugach (1995) states that these programs "represent a shift in location and an addition of activities rather than a fundamental change in the dominant attitude about teaching and learning" (p. 216). Thus, add-on inclusion programs convey the message that "inclusion, like its predecessor mainstreaming, is essentially a function of what the field of special education is already doing" (p. 218). Pugach states that if we are to realize the full potential of inclusion, we must move beyond add-on models. More effective approaches to service delivery are developed as general and special educators work collaboratively to transform and reinvent general education to better meet the needs of all students. In these new, inclusive models, changes must occur in four key elements of schooling, otherwise the changes are very likely to be superficial and ineffective. These areas are as follows:

- *Curriculum and instruction.* At the very least, adaptations must be made in what is expected of students in the classroom, how instruction is delivered, and how student progress is evaluated. In some instances, dramatic changes occur in the curriculum and classroom instruction, where the curriculum is more student centered and instruction is built upon active student involvement in learning. These issues are discussed in more detail in Chapter 6.

- *Teacher roles and responsibilities.* In well-developed inclusive schools, what teachers do as they go about their professional responsibilities changes in significant ways. They work with different students in different ways (for example, classroom teachers work with more students with disabilities, and their students work more often in cooperative groups or in peer tutoring arrangements), and they collaborate with other professionals or perhaps coteach to determine the most effective approaches for meeting the needs of all students.

- *Classroom and school organization.* In well-developed inclusive schools, the school day may be reorganized (for example, developing a block schedule in a high school), or classroom organization may change (for example, children may work together and provide assistance to one another during significant portions of the school day). These types of changes are made as teachers and administrators work to use resources more efficiently to better meet the needs of ALL students in the school.

- *Teacher beliefs about schooling.* As discussed in Chapter 4, inclusive schools work to the extent that teachers believe they are beneficial for students. To achieve an effective inclusive school, teachers must examine their beliefs about students with disabilities, inclusion, how students should be taught, what students should learn, and a range of other issues that may influence their support for these programs.

Pugach (1995) suggests that in these transformed classrooms and schools, what counts as special may not always stand out: "One measure might be the degree to which observers cannot tell, and do not need to be interested in, which students were formerly labeled as having a disability" (p. 220). In addition, in these settings it might be expected that "each student might need to spend time in a small group to get . . . assistance" (p. 220).

Improving Schools for *All* Students

As teachers and administrators progress in their discussions concerning inclusion, they often reach two conclusions regarding how schools must change. First, they conclude that this change must address the needs of *all* students, not just those with disabilities. Many students do not fit into traditional general education classrooms and schools, and inclusion must be about how schools and classrooms become more accommodating of this diversity. The following comments from two elementary teachers in a well-developed inclusive school program illustrate this point.

> Meeting the needs of all students is much bigger than meeting the needs of students with special needs. I think that many people still believe that the identified students are students who require the greatest amount of time from their teachers. I have seen all too many times that the students with the greatest needs are not identified.
>
> The hardest task for any classroom teacher is meeting the needs of all students. A classroom, whether or not it is considered "inclusive," will always have a differentiated range of abilities in which adaptations must be made in order for learning to occur . . . adaptations cannot occur only to curriculum, but must also occur in the environment and attitudes.

Second, "inclusion" is transformed to become "school improvement," because the changes relate to improving general education classrooms so that teachers are better equipped to meet the needs of all students. Thus, inclusion is no longer about "special" education for a "special" group of students, but it is about improving the education of ALL students. The following comment from an elementary teacher in a well-developed inclusive school illustrates this point.

> There is really no difference in the way that students with and without disabilities are provided with support or adaptations in the classroom. All students who need assistance or adaptations receive them from one of the adults or peers in the classroom, regardless of whether or not they are identified.

When these types of change do not occur, and inclusion programs are cast as simply focusing on special education students and programs, general education teachers are much less supportive of these programs. For example, many general educators are skeptical regarding making the major changes that are required in their classrooms for a small group of "special education" students whom they have perhaps seldom seen and for whom they bear little responsibility. Reasonable questions that general education teachers should ask regarding these programs include: How will "average" students be influenced by these programs? How will students who are learning slowly, but not labeled with a disability, be influenced? How will high-achieving students be influenced? In addition, placing emphasis solely (or largely) on students with disabilities increases the probability that special education teachers will continue to be perceived as being responsible for making the changes that are necessary and for providing support for "their" students, even when they are placed in a general education classroom.

We have found that general education classroom teachers are much more responsive to school change when it addresses improvements to their school and classrooms to better meet the needs of *all* students, *including* students with disabilities. This approach recognizes the perspective of classroom teachers, who must be responsible for all the students in their classrooms, not just the girls, those with brown hair, or those with disabilities. Also, general education teachers are acutely aware that every year, as they open the doors to their classrooms, an increasingly diverse group of students walks in. Thus, they are already pressured to determine methods to meet the different needs of students. Focusing on this requirement, and adding students with disabilities to the mix, is a way to meet the needs of students with disabilities as well as providing needed support for classroom teachers.

Empowering Schools to Manage Change

To achieve the substantive changes that are required for a well-developed inclusive program, teachers and administrators in a local school must support or "own" these changes. If this is to occur, the primary decision makers regarding these changes must be the teachers who work most closely with children and who will be responsible for implementing the changes. Fullan (1993) provides insight into the need to empower schools to manage their own change when he states that "You can't mandate what matters" (p. 22). He goes on to note that some changes that are not substantive can be mandated, if they do not require thinking or skill to implement and if they can be monitored through close and constant surveillance. Individualized education programs (IEPs) are an excellent example of this type of change. It is quite possible to mandate that teachers and multidisciplinary teams (MDTs) write out IEPs. This act can be monitored by simply reviewing the forms that result from MDT meetings. However, ensuring that the individualized program is implemented in the classroom is another matter entirely. Extensive evidence reveals that IEPs have not been implemented for students with disabilities in many cases, both in special education classrooms and in general education settings (Haynes & Jenkins, 1986; McGill-Franzen & Allington, 1991; Pugach & Warger, 1993; Smith, 1990; Wesson & Deno, 1989).

In each of the settings where the successful development of inclusive schools has taken place, teachers and building-level administrators were given the power to determine the nature and scope of changes that would be made in their setting and the power to manage this change. This did not always result in changes that were perceived as "ideal" from the perspective of the outside consultants or central administration. However, all participants recognized that ownership for the inclusive school would occur only if the local school teachers and administrators were given the power to determine the nature and scope of this change.

Tailoring Change to Each School

Change in schools—especially in special education—has long been viewed as identifying an innovation or "model" that is perceived to be "proven effective," such as individually guided education (Klausmeier, 1975), the alternative learning environments model (Wang, 1987; Wang & Birch, 1984), or mainstream assistance teams (Fuchs, Fuchs, Harris, & Roberts, 1996), and implementing (or mandating) the model in a school. Such an approach to school change fails to recognize the complexity of schools, as well as the power of teachers and local administrators in determining when and how schools are substantively changed. Goodman (1995) suggests that these innovations result in "change without difference," as they serve only to reinforce the "underlying values, power relationships, and learning experiences embedded within the conventional ways of educating children" (p. 3).

The futility of this "fidelity" (Fullan & Stiegelbauer, 1991) approach to change was recently illustrated by Fuchs, Fuchs, Harris, and Roberts (1996) as they reported on the implementation of mainstream assistance teams (MATs) in 34 elementary schools in Nashville, Tennessee. These university faculty had worked with local schools for four years as part of a federal project to develop and implement building-based support teams, or MATs. The MATs were designed to provide consultative support to teachers in addressing the needs of difficult-to-teach students. Although some of the particulars regarding the MATs evolved over the four-year project period based on feedback from teachers and administrators, the investigators sought to implement a single MAT model in each of the schools (ensuring "treatment fidelity" or that the same model was used in each school), without consideration of differences in cultures, teacher beliefs, and so forth across the schools. Furthermore, each MAT was built upon the investigators' perspective regarding effective instruction and the use of a behavioral consultation model, which they perceived (and, indeed, demonstrated) to be effective.

In their final investigation of the MATs in Nashville, they demonstrated that local educators could effectively run these building-based teams without assistance and that the teams were effective in helping teachers address the needs of many difficult-to-teach students (Fuchs et al., 1996). Thus, as the four project years ended, the investigators left the school system with a model that was proven effective; with 150 general educators, special educators, school psychologists, and guidance counselors in 34 elementary schools who were trained in the use of the model; and with ". . . a comprehensive MAT handbook written expressly for practitioners" (p. 261).

The investigators followed up on the MATs during the next school year and noted that after the "federal monies ran out and we stopped helping to organize the MATs, we failed to find one instance of MAT use" (p. 261). In explaining why the MATs were not maintained in the schools, they placed much of the blame on local administrators and asked the question, "When Will the Leaders Lead?" (p. 264). They go on to state that they anticipated that if the MATs were empirically demonstrated to be effective, the district should then "require, or at least strongly encourage, all elementary and middle schools to establish MATs" (p. 265).

The results of this investigation are quite predictable. Indeed, it would not be improper to suggest that had administrators mandated the MATs, they still would not have been faithfully implemented in the schools (i.e., there might have been teams called MATs, but "treatment fidelity" would have been lacking). In contrast to their perspective, it seems likely that the MATs failed because they represented superficial rather than substantive school change (Goodman, 1995) and because they violate many of the basic tenets of effective school change (Fullan, 1993; Goodman, 1995; Sarason, 1990). For example, schools are simply too complex to expect that a single blueprint for building-based teams will work across 34 elementary schools. In addition, the teams were based on the beliefs and values of the outside investigators (that is, their belief in the use of behavioral consultation and their perception regarding "effective instruction"), not of the teachers in the local schools.

A "model" for school change that can be implemented across a number of schools does not really exist; rather, it appears that inclusive schools differ from school to school, depending on the beliefs, values, and understandings of teachers and administrators regarding how students should be taught, what they should be taught, how the school is organized to deliver instruction, and so forth. Thus, inclusive schools must be individually tailored to the unique qualities of a given school. This tailoring often results in differences in inclusion across grade levels in an elementary school, teams in a middle school, or subject areas in a high school. For example, teachers will implement inclusion in different ways, depending upon issues such as

- Whether teachers team teach or one teacher is responsible for a classroom.
- Teacher beliefs about effective instruction, which may range from traditional, skill-based instruction to a constructivist perspective.
- How students are placed in classrooms; for example, multi-age/grade classes versus single-grade-level classes.
- Thematic instruction in math and science in a high school versus instruction in a single content area.

Resistance Is to Be Expected

Whenever significant change is undertaken, no one knows for sure that the change will be effective and that students will benefit from the changes. Developing inclusive programs is no different, although it is perhaps more risky than many forms of school change, as teachers and administrators are asked to make changes in everything they do and to make substantive changes, not simply changes that add onto what they are already doing. In addition, teachers may have had negative experiences in the past in attempting to teach students with disabilities, and now they are being asked to take these students back into their classroom under circumstances that are ill-defined at best. These circumstances should lead anyone involved in developing an inclusive program to expect that resistance would arise from many quarters. Indeed, it is surprising when strong resistance, or at least serious questions about a proposed inclusive program, does *not* develop. Teachers and administrators *should* ask questions and remain skeptical about such changes, to the extent that they are concerned about maintaining high-quality educational programs for their students. The only reason such resistance would not occur is that the changes being proposed are superficial and will not result in significant changes in the professional lives of teachers and administrators.

Related to this issue, some research reveals that teachers who are most resistant to inclusion, at least initially, are the most effective teachers in a school (Gersten, Walker, & Darch, 1988). Upon reflection, it seems obvious that this would be the case. As Gersten and colleagues (1988) note, these are teachers who use their instructional time most efficiently; thus, their concerns regarding adding students with disabilities to their classrooms most likely result from fears that they will not maintain high levels of student academic performance. As noted in Chapter 4, most of the issues that teachers raise regarding inclusion are logical and justified, and they must be addressed before inclusive programs can be successfully implemented.

A final consideration regarding teacher and administrator "resistance" is that those who question changes are often viewed as "the enemy" and as being unduly resistant or slow to change. Taking this perspective is not productive, and it casts resistance as an "attitude" problem rather than as the natural reaction of professionals to change . . . change that is always wrought with anxiety, frustration, and tension. As Fullan and Miles (1992) state,

21

Blaming "resistance" for the slow pace of reform also keeps us from understanding that individuals and groups faced with something new need to assess the change for its genuine possibilities and for how it bears on their self-interest (p. 748).

In sum, changes that are made in a school when inclusive programs are being developed simply cannot be limited to special education programs and students with disabilities. On a technical level, it can be argued that schools are too interconnected and that changes in one part of the system influence too many other parts of the system for isolated changes in special education to work. Perhaps a more important reason to examine changes in the entire school as an inclusive program is being developed is that the changes being proposed promise to benefit a large proportion of the school population. Moreover, these programs are designed to provide the classroom teacher with support that is necessary to accommodate diversity in the general education classroom, including students labeled with disabilities and those who are not so labeled. Indeed, students who do not fit the expectations of the general education classroom should benefit from a well-developed inclusive program. This includes students who are not labeled with a formal disability but who learn more slowly (or more rapidly) than other students, students who are more active or less attentive than other students, and a range of others who don't fit the typical pattern of expectations in the general education classroom. As many teachers and principals have told us, a well-developed inclusive program results in better instruction for all students, not just those with disabilities.

2 The Need for Leadership and Collaboration in Developing Inclusive Schools

As Chapter 1 illustrates, the development and implementation of an inclusive program requires major changes in an entire school, significantly influencing the daily lives of teachers, administrators, and students. To achieve such changes, strong leadership is needed within the local school. This chapter addresses the leadership that is necessary to develop and implement a successful inclusive school program. First, we look at the need for strong leadership from the school principal. Next, we discuss the need for support from both the administration and teachers, if school change is to be successful. Then, we review the types of leadership required as successful school change is achieved. Finally, there is a discussion of the need for collaboration and team building in developing and implementing a successful plan for school change and inclusion.

The Importance of the Building Principal

The most influential person in developing inclusive schools is the building principal. If the principal indicates that the timing is not right for developing an inclusive school, there is little to no chance that an inclusive school will be developed. Simply put, an inclusive school cannot be successfully implemented without the *active* support of the building principal. We have come to feel so strongly about this issue that we will not work with a local school in developing an inclusive school unless the building principal is actively involved in planning the changes. Moreover, when we are approached to work with a school to develop an inclusive program, the first person we want to talk with is the building principal. In our first meeting with the principal, we attempt to convey the idea that developing an inclusive school does not just relate to program changes for students with disabilities but requires extensive changes in the entire school. Following this background discussion about inclusion, we ask the principal if he or she thinks the school faculty would be interested in developing a more inclusive school. If so, we ask if the principal would be willing to actively participate with teachers and other stakeholders as they develop and implement the required changes. If, at any point in this discussion, the principal reveals anything less than strong support for inclusion, we begin to doubt whether a successful inclusive school can be developed.

Let us be perfectly clear about what is being said here: We are not suggesting that a building principal's refusal to actively support the development and implementation of an inclusive school is necessarily a bad decision. The principal may have a very good reason for such a refusal. For example, there may be limited support for developing such a program from general education teachers in the building. Special education teachers may be strongly opposed to developing such a program. Other major initiatives may result in a "full plate" for the school, not allowing the time and energy necessary for developing a successful inclusive school. Whatever the reason, the principal is the key person who makes the initial decision regarding whether the time is right for developing an inclusive school.

Top-Down and Bottom-Up Change

Change can be initiated by anyone in a setting—a teacher or group of teachers, a principal or central office administrator, or a parent. However, to be successful, change ultimately must be supported by the administration (top-down support) as well as by the teachers who must implement the change (bottom-up support). Administrative support (especially from the building principal) for developing and implementing inclusive schools is important for a number of reasons, as administrators provide an atmosphere that is conducive to change and provide teachers with a range of substantive supports that are necessary for change. Support from the central administration also is important in many ways, such as

- Providing resources for the development of the inclusive program, including release time for planning, staff development, and support for visits to model inclusive programs in other school districts.
- Supporting the development of the program and the related risk-taking with parents, school board members, and other stakeholders.

The support of teachers for the changes involved in developing and implementing inclusive schools is needed because these changes simply will not occur if teachers are not supportive. Developing and implementing inclusive school programs is certainly among the most complex change endeavors being undertaken in schools today. It is perhaps a cliché to state that teachers must own a change if it is to be successful; however, that is certainly the case with inclusive school programs. Research on teachers' perspectives on inclusion provides a number of issues that must be addressed to assuage teacher fears (and ensure their support) regarding the development and implementation of inclusive school programs, including the following:

- Who will be included.
- Whether students will benefit from inclusion.
- Whether students with disabilities will have a negative effect on the classroom.
- How the classroom teacher's role and responsibilities will be influenced.
- Whether the classroom teacher will have the necessary time, resources, and/or expertise to make inclusion successful.

Two primary approaches will ease teachers' fears and ensure that they support inclusion. One is to ensure them that they will be the primary decision makers regarding the inclusive school—for example, who will be included, under what circumstances they will be included, and so forth. This decision making must, of course, include all teachers who will be involved in implementing the inclusive school, not simply a subgroup (e.g., special education teachers). A second approach that is useful is to give teachers the opportunity to visit schools where such programs are in place, so they can see firsthand that successful inclusive schools can be developed. Teachers can observe in classrooms and talk with other teachers and administrators about the logistics of developing and implementing an inclusive school, as well as the rewards and challenges involved in an ongoing program.

Several Types of Leadership Required

When we began to work with faculty, administrators, and other stakeholders to develop inclusive schools, we recognized the importance of leadership in this process. We also recognized that change must be both top-down and bottom-up. However, we did not fully recognize how important this leadership was. Nor did we realize that different types of leadership would be required from different stakeholders in a building if successful inclusive schools were to be developed. Of course, as previously noted, the most important leadership in a building is provided by the principal. If a successful inclusive school is to be developed, the principal must be actively involved in developing and implementing the plan. We have attempted to work with teams that have "kept the principal informed" about progress, but, in our experience, this has *never* worked as well as having the principal involved as an active participant. The building principal simply has too much at stake not to be involved when major school change is undertaken.

This leadership is critical for several reasons, the most important of which is that the principal, as the instructional leader in the building, must be fully informed and have active input about any major change in the school, and the implementation of an inclusive school will certainly require major changes. Leadership from the principal regarding inclusion is also important for scores of other reasons, including the need to

- Promote and model support for inclusion and the need for changes with the school staff.
- Provide necessary support for program development and implementation, including
  - Time for planning
  - Staff development needed to implement changes
  - Resources needed to support changes
- Ensure that teachers are in control of changes.
- Ensure that the local school faculty own and support changes.
- Ensure that the inclusive school is tailored to the needs of the local setting.
- Encourage risk-taking among teachers and assure teachers that they will be given support if certain aspects of the inclusive school do not initially succeed.
- Support teachers involved in developing and implementing the needed changes, especially with other teachers, parents, and central administration.
- Encourage ongoing evaluation and improvement of the inclusive school.

Although the principal is the most important leader, others must provide leadership if success is to be realized. For example, teachers are closest to the students who will be influenced by the changes that are made, and they must advocate for these changes with the students and their parents. It is also important to keep in mind that teachers often must change their professional role and activities to ensure that inclusion is successful. Under these circumstances, it is critical that teachers provide leadership in conveying to other teachers in the building, as well as to parents and building administration, that they are willing to undertake the necessary changes and that they feel these changes will benefit children and be worth the effort.

A third type of leadership needed for successful school change is someone who has a good grasp of the process of change and how to progress through this process to a successful conclusion. This person may be the principal, a teacher, a school psychologist or counselor, or an "outsider." The person must understand a great deal about school change (e.g., much of what is included in this book), how to build teams that work well together, how to solve problems that will inevitably arise, and generally how to foster collaborative relationships. The authors have served in this role in some schools, where we worked as facilitators for change and made suggestions about both the process and substance of change, but final decisions regarding what would change and how changes would occur were made by the stakeholders in the local school.

A final type of leadership found to be very useful is one or more persons whom the authors have come to call "keepers of the vision." These persons must be very knowledgeable about inclusion, and throughout the process of developing and implementing the inclusive school they continue to remind others why it is important to take on such a task, what the goals of inclusion are, what types of change need to occur, how all students will benefit from the changes that will occur, how inclusion will benefit students with disabilities, and so forth. A keeper of the vision will often become the leading advocate for inclusion in the building and will work to sell the program to other teachers in the building as well as to parents, students, or administrators who have questions or concerns about inclusion. For us, the building principal or a special education teacher most often serves in this role, although general education teachers occasionally take on this function.

Collaboration and Team Building Are Essential

The following comments from a middle school special education teacher address the need for collaboration to effectively include students with disabilities in general education classrooms.

EXAMPLE

> The most striking thing I remember about starting to get some of my kids into general education classes was the stress that it created for me. I was very comfortable teaching these students in my class. I had an assistant and only six or eight students at a time, so I could

—continued—

EXAMPLE

—continued—

structure the class and help students focus on the academic content they needed to learn. When I began to work with teachers who had 25 or 30 students in their class, with no assistant, addressing a content I didn't know much about—I have to admit, I didn't know quite what to do. I'd never taught in a class with that large a group of students. Although I had a strong background in math, I didn't know much about the other content areas, the curricula that were used in the classrooms or how general education classrooms were organized to deliver this content to so many students.

One student I remember in particular, Joe, had behavior problems . . . actually he was labeled ADHD and also had a reading disability. I talked with an English teacher who had a very structured class about including Joe in her class. Joe did okay for the first week or so, but then he began to act out and seek attention, and had trouble paying attention, especially in cooperative groups. I observed the class several times, and then the teacher and I met. She expected that I would have some answers for her regarding how to "control" Joe's behavior as well as how to adapt the content of the class. I admitted to her right off that I had only taught Joe in a small group of no more than seven other students and I often had another teacher or assistant in the classroom. I had some ideas about how to deal with his behavior in her classroom, but I really wasn't sure how my ideas would work in a classroom that included 30 other students. Telling the teacher this really helped. We both realized that while neither of us knew exactly what to do to help Joe, the best thing we could do was to put our heads together and come up with some ideas.

If the truth be told, no one *alone* knows how to develop and implement an inclusive school program or how to make an inclusive classroom work. For example, good inclusive classrooms require the combined expertise of the general education teacher (an expert in the content being taught as well as how to deliver that content to large groups) and the special education teacher (an expert in adapting content for individual student needs and delivering instruction to students who lack certain basic skills). The same can be said for the major changes that are required in a school. The combined ideas and expertise of general education teachers, special education teachers, and administrators are required to develop an inclusive school. This sharing of expertise ensures that many of the problems associated with such changes are recognized and that the best available solutions to the problems are identified.

This need for collaboration requires that a team of teachers, administrators, and other stakeholders be formed to put together a plan for inclusion in a given school. This team benefits the inclusive school in many ways, including the following:

- The team provides leadership in developing, implementing, evaluating, and maintaining the inclusive program.
- Team members provide a foundation upon which to build the inclusive school.
- The inclusive school that is developed is more likely to be tailored to the individual needs of the school.
- Teachers and building administrators are much more likely to support and "own" the inclusive school that has been developed.
- Teachers develop collaborative skills through team building, as they learn to work together, share expertise, and solve problems.
- Teachers build professional relationships and develop skills that make collaboration (such as coteaching) easier as the inclusive program is implemented.

Fox and Ysseldyke (1997) recently provided an excellent example of an inclusive program developed and implemented in the absence of collaboration between general and special education teachers. These investigators conducted a case study of a middle school as it attempted to implement an inclusive program. A plan for the inclusive program was developed by special education teachers with the assistance of a liaison from the district-level inclusion committee. This plan was then " . . . approved by the district administration and therefore constituted the district's intentions about how inclusion was to be implemented at the middle school" (p. 88). This approach to school change predictably resulted in a program that evidenced little interaction " . . . between the included students and the general education teacher or between the included and other students" (p. 91). Further, "General education teachers varied in the amount of effort they made to include the students with (disabilities)" (p. 91). In sum, "Major changes in teaching strategies to accommodate the included students did not occur" (p. 91), and the special education teacher and students remained largely isolated in the general education classroom.

One final comment regarding collaboration: Although coteaching is not required as part of an inclusive school, the authors have found that such close relationships between teachers benefit inclusive schools immeasurably. These relationships allow general and special education teachers the opportunity to learn about and from one another in ways that are not available when the special education teacher only observes or works in the general education classroom occasionally and provides only consultation services to the general education teacher. In addition, coteaching allows teachers the opportunity to naturally share expertise regarding students, communicate regarding curriculum and instruction on an ongoing basis, and coordinate activities in the classroom. Finally, coteaching often provides a more professionally satisfying role for the special education teacher, who works as an equal partner with the general education teacher.

In sum, leadership from the principal, as well as from many others both inside and outside the local school, is required if successful inclusive programs are to be developed. The many types of leadership required for school change that are described in this chapter illustrate the complexity of such changes. However, we have found that a strong leader or two in a building can go a long way toward ensuring that change does occur. Perhaps the best description we can provide is that strong leadership is contagious: Others soon want to become involved in the changes in their school and are more likely to take risks if strong leadership for the changes is obvious.

Schoolwide Issues in Creating Inclusive Schools

While the previous chapters address big issues regarding school change and leadership that are crucial to the successful development of inclusive schools, several nuts-and-bolts issues also must be addressed as these programs are being developed, implemented, and maintained. This chapter addresses these highly specific, yet critically important, issues:

- The need for adequate planning time.
- The need for professional development.
- Understanding the uniqueness of the special education teacher's role.
- The need to balance the desire for "natural proportion" with intensity of services.
- Providing careful consideration to scheduling and use of resources.
- Considerations in maintaining an inclusive school.

The Need for Adequate Planning Time

When considering the complexity of changes that are required to develop an inclusive school, it is important to keep in mind that program development and implementation will take a large amount of time, energy, and other resources (Fox & Ysseldyke, 1997; Fullan, 1993). Teacher and administrator time is needed to plan the inclusive school, visit other successful inclusive school programs, engage in staff development, and a plethora of other activities. Later,

Chapter 9 describes a systematic approach to developing inclusive schools that vividly illustrates this point. The 10 steps we have used when working with many schools require intensive use of resources. This process will take at least six months to complete, and it often takes a full year or longer. Considering the time demands that will be placed on teachers and administrators in developing and implementing an inclusive school, it is important that these responsibilities not simply be added on to the other responsibilities of these busy and often overworked professionals. Although the nature of the support teachers and administrators receive will vary greatly depending on the local school system, resources must be available to ensure adequate support for planning meetings, professional development, visits to other schools, and so forth.

In additional to this need for planning time as the inclusive program is being developed, it is also at least as important (and perhaps more important) to provide ongoing planning time *after* the program is implemented to ensure success. For example, after implementing an inclusive program, teachers who coteach or otherwise collaborate will need to meet to discuss and plan their collaborative activities. Furthermore, a team of stakeholders should continue to meet to evaluate and adjust the inclusive program as needed. (This issue will be discussed in more detail later in this chapter.) Thus, planning time is a critical issue in ensuring the development, as well as the maintenance, of a successful inclusive school.

The Need for Professional Development

To ensure that teachers are well prepared for successfully developing and implementing an inclusive school, sufficient opportunities for professional development must be provided. As Fox and Ysseldyke (1997) suggest, professional development is especially important as inclusive schools are being developed and implemented, considering the fact that teachers are being asked " . . . to accept new responsibilities and to expand their roles into . . . new and, perhaps, personally threatening areas" (p. 96). Moreover, as noted in Chapter 1, the necessary changes are not simply added on to the current school program but rather require significant changes in how teachers work. These changes require that teachers gain new understandings of teaching and learning as well as the new skills that are needed to ensure that they are well prepared to implement the required changes.

Bull and Buechler (1997) offer several principles that we have found quite useful for ensuring that professional development activities are tailored to the individual needs of the local school and are successful in preparing teachers for the changes being implemented. We suggest that effective professional development

- Is school based.
- Uses coaching and other follow-up procedures.
- Is collaborative.
- Is embedded in the daily lives of teachers, providing for continuous growth.
- Focuses on student learning and is evaluated at least in part on that basis.

While professional development activities must be tailored to the individual needs of the local school, we have found that most schools benefit from visits to sites where inclusive schools have been successfully developed and from participating in situation-specific problem-solving sessions (Roach, 1995). In addition, there are several topics that often need to be addressed, including the following:

- Why implement an inclusive school? How will it work? How *well* will it work?
- Collaboration, teaming, and coteaching.
- Instructional strategies and curricular adaptations.
- Alternative grouping strategies (e.g., cooperative learning, multi-age grouping, peer tutoring).
- Understanding the change process.
- Schoolwide discipline, conflict resolution, and social skills training.

Finally, continuing professional development is not only important in ensuring that teachers gain the necessary skills to successfully implement an inclusive school, it also offers *all* teachers in a school the opportunity to learn about inclusion and school change and to collaborate with others in determining how the school and classrooms will be changed to more successfully accommodate student diversity. The involvement of the school faculty in continuing professional development thus makes it more likely that ownership for the inclusive school will be broad-based among the teaching staff.

The Special Education Teacher's Role

As we have worked with schools in implementing inclusive programs, one of the major concerns has been the dramatic changes that have occurred in the roles of special education teachers and the significantly increased responsibilities that have been placed on these professionals. As one elementary teacher commented after working in a newly developed inclusive program,

> I support inclusion, but I don't know if I'll keep teaching if things don't change. I enjoyed my self-contained class. I had my own students, my own classroom, my own materials and curriculum. When we went to inclusion, I lost my classroom, my students, and everything. I don't have control over anything anymore. I also have to adapt my teaching style to four other teachers I work with, as I go into *their* classrooms, with *their* students, *their* curriculum. Then I have to learn the curriculum across three different grade levels! It's tough. Why doesn't anyone adapt to *my* teaching style?

We have found that variations on this teacher's experience are not unusual for special education teachers. In many settings, these teachers have worked with anywhere from three to eight other professionals, and, under the best of conditions (e.g., true collaboration, time for coteaching), the job is still extraordinarily challenging. Providing a rewarding, professionally satisfying role for the special education teachers should be a priority of an inclusive school. For example, it is important to limit the number of teachers a special education teacher is expected to work with and the number of grade levels at which the teacher is expected to work. Furthermore, it is important that the special education teacher has a professionally appropriate role in the general education classroom; these teachers typically want to provide direct instruction to students, and they desire a role in the classroom as an equal with other professionals.

Many problems arise when special education teachers do not have a professionally satisfying role. An immediate problem that arises is that an important resource for students is not being used well, and thus the students' needs are not being met as well as they should be. Related to this problem, any professional is going to be more successful if she/he feels that she/he is contributing to the success of students and is viewed as a productive professional by peers. Finally, if a special educator remains in a role that is inappropriate, burnout becomes a distinct possibility and she/he may seek other roles in the school or in other professions to reduce the pressure and stress of the job.

Balancing the Desire for Natural Proportion with Appropriate Intensity of Services

As we began to work with a Midwestern school district several years ago, they were struck by the large proportion of students with disabilities in some schools and the small proportion in others. As they examined these data and worked with the schools more closely, they found that many students with disabilities in this district were being bused to schools to "ensure efficient service delivery." Overall, one-third of the students with mild disabilities (learning disabilities and mild mental retardation) were educated in the school they would have attended if they were not labeled with a disability, while the other two-thirds were bused away from their neighborhood. Looking at the patterns of student placement over a period of years, we also discovered that the proportion of students in a given school changed over time, sometimes abruptly. These changes occurred because students in special education classes were routinely moved from one building to another when the need for additional classroom space arose. Administrators who made these decisions reasoned that most of the students with disabilities were not in their neighborhood schools anyway, so it would make little difference to move them to another school. In one instance, a separate class for students with learning disabilities had moved five times, from one school to another, over the course of seven years. This practice caused significant difficulty for schools as they attempted to develop inclusive schools, not to mention the unstable school environment that many students with disabilities experienced.

In this school district, we spent two years developing and implementing a plan for moving students with disabilities back to their neighborhood schools before they began to work with schools to develop inclusive programs. There were simply too many students with disabilities in some schools to include them all, and in other schools there were so few students with disabilities that no special education teacher was assigned to the school. Still other schools had a relatively large number of students one year and relatively few students the next. As these issues were discussed in this school district, all agreed that much greater success could be achieved in developing inclusive schools if the students were first moved back to their neighborhood schools.

In general, students with disabilities should go to the school they would attend if they did not have a disability. This results in a natural proportion of students with disabilities in a given school. For example, in an elementary school with 500 students, if 11 percent of the students in the district are identified with disabilities, it would be anticipated that about 55 students with disabilities would be found. In addition to ensuring natural proportions, providing an education in the neighborhood school has many additional advantages for students with disabilities:

- Avoiding long rides on buses to distant schools.
- Going to school with the same students who live in the student's neighborhood, attend local churches, shop in local stores, and so forth.
- Involvement of parents in the local school.
- A feeling of ownership by the teachers and administration of the local school for *all* students who live in the school's catchment area.

- Stability in school placement; that is, a student is moved only because of redistricting, which affects all students.

Once a natural proportion of students with disabilities is in a school, we found that strict adherence to this principle is not possible on a classroom-by-classroom basis. To illustrate, if the 55 students in the elementary school of 500 students described previously were spread equally across grades 1–5, with 11 students per grade level, and there were four classes per grade level, one would expect that 2 or 3 students with disabilities would be in each classroom. We have found that this approach does not work for several reasons.

First and foremost, all students with disabilities do not place equal demands on teachers for assistance and support. Some students are extremely demanding, require much teacher time for individual work, or disrupt classroom activities with some regularity. In contrast, other students with disabilities place few demands on a teacher and require little support or assistance. Simply put, some students with disabilities require intense support in the general education classroom, while others require much less support. To illustrate, a teacher we have worked with for several years recently stated that she had one student with a disability in her class, and he was so demanding that she could not take on any additional students with disabilities. In previous years this same teacher had taken on four or five students with disabilities in her classroom with few problems. The differing needs of students with disabilities for support require flexibility in scheduling by the special education staff and make it difficult—indeed, in our experience, undesirable—to have a natural proportion of students with disabilities in every classroom.

A second issue regarding the principle of natural proportion is that, no matter what level of training and support for inclusion exists in a building, some teachers are going to be more tolerant of student differences and better prepared and able to adapt to a diverse range of students in their classroom. Thus, some teachers will run a classroom that is well designed to meet the needs of a diverse range of students and will be able to meet the needs of five students with disabilities, while other teachers will not be able to achieve this goal with the same five students and the same level of support.

A third issue when considering natural proportion is that some students with disabilities require an intensity of services that is very difficult to deliver in a general education classroom, especially if students with disabilities are in neighborhood schools, and thus spread in a natural proportion across schools in a school district. For example, we have worked in one school district for the past 10 years in developing, implementing, monitoring, and improving inclusive schools. Currently, at the elementary level across 14 schools, students with the most challenging behaviors are bused to two schools, one on each side of town. Most of these students are aggressive and highly disruptive in general education classrooms and were found to be very difficult to include successfully in their neighborhood school. Consequently, these students are clustered into two schools so that appropriate intensity of services can be provided to support them in a separate special education classroom for part of the school day and sufficient resources are available to support them in general education classrooms for part of the school day.

A final issue regarding natural proportion and intensity of services relates to the resources that are available to provide support to students with disabilities in a given school. Because of limits on resources, we have found that it is often necessary to balance the need for intensity of services with the guiding principle of natural proportion in considering student placements—that is, the closer a school moves toward natural proportion in classrooms, the more difficult it is to deliver intense supports to some students. For example, in a high school we worked in, a limited number of team-taught, content-area classes were offered. These classes often included up to 10 students with disabilities, along with 20 students who were not labeled and two teachers, a general education content-area teacher and a special education teacher. Considering the resources available in this school, the other demands that were placed on the special education teachers (e.g., teaching learning strategy classes, providing support in job settings), and the average class size (over 30), the best option available—which provided the intensity of services necessary to meet student needs and came as close to natural proportion as possible—was to include this high proportion (up to one-third) of students with disabilities in general education classrooms.

Thus, while natural proportion is an excellent guiding principle for student placement in schools and classrooms, it is undesirable to attempt to strictly adhere to this principle on a classroom-by-classroom basis. Moreover, balancing the need for natural proportion with the need for intense support for some students with disabilities provides a more realistic approach for meeting the needs of all students with disabilities in inclusive settings.

Scheduling and Use of Resources

Related to the issues regarding natural proportion and intensity of services, careful consideration must be given in an inclusive school to how resources are used and how the school day is scheduled. Concerning the use of resources, a comment that we frequently hear in the initial stages of developing an inclusive school is, "We don't have enough special education teachers to develop a successful inclusive school." The problem with this comment is that inclusive schools are being viewed by the speaker as *solely* a special education issue. One of the most important issues to keep in mind when developing an inclusive school is that these programs should address the need to provide a better education for *all* students in a school; thus, as the inclusive school is being developed, *all* of the resources in a school should be examined, not just resources that are viewed as "special education." Thus, Title I teachers, class-size aides, remedial aides, volunteers, custodians, secretaries, teachers of every kind, principals, preservice teachers, and any other resources in the setting should be examined to ensure the most efficient use of resources to meet the needs of all students.

In our experience and that of others (Fox & Ysseldyke, 1997; Fullan, 1993), local school personnel often underestimate the resources (e.g., time, energy, money) that will be required to develop and implement an inclusive school. Thus, administrators, teachers, and other stakeholders in a school must spend time searching for resources and actively exploring methods to more effectively and efficiently use the resources that exist within the school. Fullan and Miles (1992) suggest that school change requires "attention not just to resources, but to 'resourcing.' The actions required are those of scanning the school and its environment for resources and matching them to existing needs; acquiring resources (buying, negotiating, or just plain grabbing); creating time through scheduling changes and other arrangements; and building local capacity through the development of such structures as steering groups, coordinating committees, and cadres of local trainers" (p. 751). These authors go on to state that "Good resourcing requires facing up to the need for funds and abjuring any false pride about self-sufficiency. Above all, it takes willingness to invent, to go outside the frame in garnering and reworking resources" (p. 751).

An issue that is strongly related to resource use is how the school day is scheduled. An elementary school principal recently told us:

> Our inclusion program has never been as good as it should have been because we had other priorities in our scheduling. Time for lunch, recess, special areas, and many other things took priority. Now we realize that the education of all students in our building must take top priority. We can provide better and more intensive services for these students if we schedule better. The tail can't wag the dog!

We have found that schools address scheduling issues in many innovative ways. For example, an elementary school we worked with decided, based on feedback they had received on statewide tests of achievement, that they needed to give language arts and mathematics top priority in their school. To use their resources as efficiently as possible, the faculty decided to schedule a two-hour block in the morning that would be used for language arts and mathematics for the primary-level students (grades 1–3), and a two-hour block in the afternoon that would be used for intermediate students (grades 4–6). This schedule allowed the opportunity to use available resources more efficiently, provided more intensive supports for students who needed them, and gave teachers the opportunity to regroup students as needed for basic skills instruction.

A second example of efficient scheduling to support an inclusive school is provided by a high school where we worked. This high school had a well-designed inclusive school in place, with a school day that was scheduled using a standard, six-period day. The faculty and administration in the school decided that longer periods of instruction would be advantageous for all students and decided to implement a block schedule. This resulted in a change from a schedule that had six 50-minute periods per day, with classes meeting daily, to a schedule with four 85-minute periods a day, with classes meeting every other day. This block schedule resulted in many advantages for all students, including more time for instruction, more class sessions with team-taught classes (using a general education and a special education teacher), instructional methods that were better suited to meeting diverse student needs (e.g., less lecture and more projects, active student involvement), and fewer discipline problems (Weller & McLeskey, in press).

When efficient use of resources is considered in a school, many other alternatives should be considered, including multi-age groupings (e.g., combining students in grades 1–3, 3–6, 7–8, or some other combination), teaming of teachers using a middle school model, coteaching using two general education teachers who combine their classes, and blocking parts of the school day for interdisciplinary instruction.

Two other issues merit discussion regarding scheduling and student placement. First, problems often arise as insufficient time and consideration are given to placement of students with disabilities in special-area classes (e.g., music). For example, at times large numbers of students with disabilities are placed in a single special-area class, while at other times special-area teachers are provided little support in adapting to meet the needs of students with disabilities in their classrooms. Simply put, special-area teachers should be involved in decision making as inclusive schools are being developed, and they should receive support and training similar to that provided to other teachers in a setting.

A final issue that must be considered is ensuring that classrooms do not have an inordinate number of students who place excessive demands on the classroom teacher. A comment from a principal from an inclusive school that has been ongoing for the past 10 years illustrates this point:

EXAMPLE

I remember the first year of our inclusion program. We had several students in the 4th grade who had problem behaviors. We also had a group of students who weren't reading very well. We had one designated inclusion class in 4th grade, and the special education teacher spent a large block of time each day in this class. We thought it was logical to put several of the students with problems in that class. They would receive the extra support of the special education teacher, and the classroom teacher was very good. It made a lot of sense on paper. The year was a disaster. The teachers just had too many needy kids in the class, and the students fed off one another. We'll *never* do that again!

Placing a large number of students who have academic or behavioral difficulties in one classroom obviously defeats the purpose of inclusion and results in another form of tracking or ability grouping of students, which should be avoided.

Maintaining an Inclusive School

In working with inclusive schools over the past 10 years, we have noted three general patterns of development of these programs:

- *Continuous improvement.* Some programs continue to improve after the first year of implementation, view the inclusive school as a "work in progress" rather than a finished product, and continue to question the program and how to make it more effective.
- *Stagnated development.* Some programs adapt as new teachers become involved in the inclusive school or as new groups of students enter the school but make few substantive changes in the inclusive school after it is initially implemented.
- *Drift toward a traditional special education program.* Still other programs, for a variety of reasons, begin to move students and teachers back toward a traditional, pull-out special education model of service delivery. This change occurs for a number of reasons,

including (1) rigidly maintaining the initial inclusive school plan, even as feedback from teachers or changes in the school make the plan unworkable or unsuccessful; (2) failing to monitor the progress of students with disabilities in the inclusive school (classroom teachers begin to feel that students with disabilities aren't making as much progress as "typical" students, that they should be making more progress, and that they would make more progress if they received specialized, special education instruction); and (3) failing to maintain an inclusion planning team, with the responsibility of monitoring and changing the inclusive school as needed.

Strategies to ensure that an inclusive school continues to improve and be successful may include the following:

1. *Maintaining an inclusion planning team, with responsibility for monitoring and suggesting changes in the inclusive school as needed.* This team should review the inclusive school at least once a year and work with the school faculty and administration to make needed changes. The most important time for making such changes is over the summer, as students are reassigned to class placements and as students and teachers move into and out of the school.

2. *Ensuring continuity among teachers who teach in the inclusive school.* We worked in one school where the teachers who teamed with the special education teachers and worked in the "inclusion classroom" at each grade level changed each year. This required that the entire inclusion program be rethought each year, as a new group of teachers, with different ideas and preferences, were involved in the program. After taking this approach for three years, the school faculty and administration decided that a few teachers would move into and out of the inclusive program each year but that it was important to maintain a core of teachers from one year to the next, ensuring continuity in the program.

3. *Continuing to provide teachers with time to plan for the ongoing, day-to-day collaboration that is such an important part of an inclusive school.* Many successful inclusive schools build time into the school day to ensure that teachers who collaborate or coteach have ample time to plan their collaborative activities and adapt to

changing student needs and curriculum requirements. This planning time improves the effectiveness of the collaborative relationship and allows teachers the opportunity to examine and change the inclusive school in their classrooms, as needed.

4. *Ongoing staff development is critical to the continued success of an inclusive school.* At times, after beginning to implement an inclusive school, teachers become aware of particular staff development needs that previously were not so obvious. Staff development support is also critical for teachers as they begin to teach in the inclusive school, as they are provided support regarding the basics of inclusion (e.g., understand the rationale behind inclusion, examine their perspective toward teaching and learning), as well as the skills that are needed to ensure program success (e.g., collaborating with others, adapting classrooms for diverse student needs).

5. *Ensuring that a plan for evaluating the inclusive school is developed and implemented.* At a minimum, such an evaluation should include

- Examining stakeholders' satisfaction with the inclusive school (e.g., ask teachers what the strengths and challenges of the inclusive school are). Stakeholders should include teachers, administrators, support personnel, students, parents, and others in the school community.
- Monitoring the academic and social/behavioral progress of students in the inclusive school.
- Ensuring that students with disabilities are full members of the learning and social communities of the school.
- Ensuring that the rhythm of the day for students with disabilities is as similar to that of other students as possible.

Finally, in our experience, once an inclusive program has been implemented, the biggest mistake that stakeholders can make is to consider it a "finished product." A good inclusive school program can *never* be more than a work in progress. Consider the following comment made by a former special education teacher who had been working as an "inclusion teacher" for five years in an inclusive school that was widely viewed as very successful:

> When we first developed our program, we really didn't know what we were doing. We tried some things that worked and some things that didn't. Now that we've been doing inclusion for five years, we have a pretty good idea about how to do it, but we keep changing our program every year, and at times more often than that, because students keep changing, teachers keep changing, and we keep figuring out how to make things work better.

Schools are simply too complex and dynamic for inclusive programs to be anything other than a work in progress. Of course, this is true of any comprehensive school change endeavor, and inclusion is certainly no exception. Moreover, schools cannot fully plan in advance the many changes needed to achieve a successful inclusive school. Some changes that seem feasible to teachers and administrators simply do not work, while changes in the school setting may occur that require changes in the inclusion plan. Consider the following example:

> The authors had been working with a school for a year, planning an inclusive program. The school had two special education teachers; one would work with the primary-level teachers, and the other would work with intermediate teachers. Students with disabilities would be clustered in one class at each grade level to simplify scheduling and allow for more intensive support for the students. In addition, the special education teachers would keep a separate classroom that they or general education teachers could use when they grouped the students for instruction, read tests to some of the students, and a variety of other instructional activities.
>
> As the school year began, the principal was surprised to find that a large number of new students had moved into the school's catchment area, and he had to hire several new teachers and use all available classrooms in the building. This resulted in several logistical issues that, in short, made the plan for inclusion unworkable. The teachers were in a panic for the first month of school, trying to work out a revised plan. By December, the teachers proudly stated that they had worked out a better plan than the original, but the process had been painful!

This circumstance may lead some to surmise that the planning the teachers and principal did was not necessary and that a plan could have been developed "on the run" as the school year began. The comments of the teachers and principal strongly suggest that this was not the case. For example, the teachers and principal in this setting stated that the planning that they did to develop their inclusive program was very beneficial for them, in spite of the fact that they were never able to implement the planned changes. They noted that these planning activities provided them with the collaboration skills that were necessary to work together to develop an alternative plan. Furthermore, these collaborative activities provided them with the opportunity to get to know each other, so that professional preferences were apparent and they developed trust in their colleagues and were willing to take risks that they otherwise might not have been willing to take.

While we have found that an extended period of time for planning is indispensable in developing an inclusive program, it is important to note that everything cannot be planned in advance, even under ideal circumstances. This circumstance led Fullan (1993) to suggest that the lack of a detailed blueprint for change forces those involved in change to look at strategic planning in a very different way, and he suggests that "Ready, fire, aim" may be a more appropriate approach to conceptualize school change.

> "Ready" is important, because there has to be some notion of direction, but it is killing to bog down the process with vision, mission, and strategic planning before you know enough about dynamic reality. "Fire" is action and inquiry, where skills, clarity, and learning are fostered. "Aim" is crystallizing new beliefs, formulating mission and vision statements, and focusing strategic planning. Vision and strategic planning come later; if anything, they come at step 3, not step 1 (pp. 31–32).

Examining Beliefs, Attitudes, and Understandings as Inclusive Schools Are Developed

W e have found that the most important place to begin planning an inclusion program is with a discussion regarding beliefs of teachers, administrators, and other stakeholders about schooling in general and inclusion in particular. What stakeholders believe often serves as a major impediment (or facilitator) to the development of successful inclusive schools. Moreover, if teachers and administrators do not recognize the need to examine and change some of their beliefs regarding inclusion and schooling, the resultant inclusive program will likely entail only superficial change, or what Goodman (1995) calls "change without difference." Consequently, the following sections address the need to consider teacher and administrator beliefs about inclusion in particular and schooling in general as they begin the development of an inclusive school program.

Teacher and Administrator Beliefs About Inclusion

Teachers and administrators invariably have many questions about inclusion as they begin to entertain the possibility of changing their school and developing inclusive programs. Typical concerns relate to questions such as the following:

- What will my role be in the inclusive program?
- What will be the impact of the inclusive program on the academic and social progress of students with disabilities?
- What will be the impact of the inclusive program on students *without* disabilities?

- Will students with disabilities have a negative impact on the general education classroom?
- Will I be given the time to plan a successful inclusive program?
- Will I be given the resources necessary to develop a successful inclusive program?
- Will I be given the opportunity to develop the expertise needed to be an effective teacher in an inclusive program?

Given this range of concerns, it should not be surprising that many teachers and administrators are cautious and often skeptical about inclusive programs. Inclusion requires many changes in the general education classroom, teacher roles, school policies, and a plethora of other factors. We have found that the vast majority of teacher concerns reflect their desire to run a successful classroom, where students benefit from the experiences provided and the teacher feels that he or she is able to successfully address student needs. With this point in mind, it seems obvious that most concerns that teachers and administrators have about inclusion are justifiable and must be responded to if a successful inclusive school is to be developed.

To explore teacher and administrator concerns regarding inclusion, as well as to reach some clarity about what inclusion is and how it will work in a local school, we often ask small groups of teachers and administrators to make two lists (this exercise was originally used by the staff of the Indiana Institute on Disability and Community at Indiana University). One list should include short descriptors of what they think inclusion is; the second, short descriptors of what they think inclusion is not (see Figure 4.1).

As the list in Figure 4.1 reveals, this exercise raises many questions about inclusion that are common concerns among teachers and administrators. While these questions, as well as the way in which inclusion is conceptualized using this list, are not ideal for every school, many of the issues that must be discussed as such programs are developed are illustrated. For example,

- Should all students who live in a school's catchment area attend their neighborhood school, regardless of the severity or nature of their disability?

—Figure 4.1—
WHAT INCLUSION MEANS (AND DOES NOT MEAN)

Inclusion Means . . .

- Students with disabilities attend their neighborhood school or the school they would attend if they were not disabled.
- Each child is in an age-appropriate general education classroom.
- Every student is accepted and regarded as a full and valued member of the class and school community.
- Special education supports are provided within the context of the general education classroom.
- All students receive an education that addresses their individual needs.
- A natural proportion of students with disabilities attends any school and classroom.
- No child is excluded on the basis of type and degree of disability.
- The school promotes cooperative/collaborative teaching arrangements.
- There is building-based planning, problem solving, and ownership of all students and programs.

Inclusion Does Not Mean . . .

- "Dumping" students with disabilities into general education classrooms without careful planning and adequate support.
- Reducing services or funding for special education services.
- Overloading any classroom with students who have disabilities or who are at risk.
- Teachers spend a disproportionate amount of time teaching or adapting curriculum for students with disabilities.
- Isolating students with disabilities socially, physically, or academically within the general education classroom.
- Jeopardizing the achievement of general education students through slower instruction or less challenging curriculum.
- Special education teachers are relegated to the role of assistant in the general education classroom.
- Forcing general and special education teachers to team together without careful planning and well-defined responsibilities.

- How are students with disabilities included in the learning and social communities of the school and classroom?
- How will the school promote cooperative/collaborative teaching arrangements?

- How will the school provide appropriate support for teachers in general education classrooms?
- How will the school ensure that students who are not labeled with disabilities benefit from the changes that are made in the school?

Much of this book addresses these issues, so additional time won't be spent commenting on them here. However, we have found that a discussion of these issues provides an excellent foundation for developing an inclusive program, and it allows teachers and administrators to begin collaborating and getting to know one another and understanding what is entailed in developing such a program.

Willingness to Teach in an Inclusive Setting

As teachers begin to develop and implement inclusive classrooms, they must be able to respond, at least tentatively, in the affirmative to the questions they have about inclusion. However, we have found that the most important factor that influences teachers' beliefs about inclusion is not the research literature on the topic but their direct experiences with inclusion. Surveys of teachers (Scruggs & Mastropieri, 1996) and our experience reveal that most teachers support the concept of inclusion—that is, students with disabilities have a basic right to be educated in general education classrooms. Our experience also reveals that far more teachers support the concept of inclusion than are willing to teach in inclusive classrooms. There seems little doubt that teachers' willingness to teach in inclusive programs is strongly influenced by their direct experience with these programs. With this in mind, often the best method to begin to address the questions teachers have about inclusion is to have them visit schools where successful inclusive programs are in place. These visits allow teachers to observe in classrooms and ask questions of other teachers who have had questions and concerns similar to their own.

It is difficult to overcome negative teacher beliefs about inclusion if the teacher has been involved in implementing a poorly designed inclusive program. In such a program, students do not benefit, the program has a negative influence on the classroom, and the teacher doesn't have the necessary time, resources, and expertise to make inclusion successful (e.g., see Baines, Baines, & Masterson, 1994). To address this issue, we have found that visits to successful inclusive schools help but often are not enough. These teachers need to be assured that they will be significantly involved in decision making about inclusion and how it will work in their classroom. They also must be assured that they will have the necessary support to develop and implement a successful inclusive classroom. Of course, all teachers should receive these assurances, but it will likely take some extra effort to convince teachers who have had negative experiences with inclusion that these promises will be kept.

Teachers' and Administrators' Beliefs About Schooling

EXAMPLE

One of the authors was chairing a panel that was discussing inclusion—how it worked, whom it worked for, and so forth. The audience was a group of teachers, parents, and administrators from several local school districts. The panel included general and special education teachers, parents, and administrators. One of the elementary teachers taught science in a departmentalized 6th grade. She expressed serious doubts about inclusion, especially in her science class. She noted that students with disabilities fall further and further behind in reading as they progress through elementary school and that by the time they get to the 6th grade, many of these students cannot read material in science texts and supplemental material that is on a 6th grade reading level (or higher). She went on to suggest that because of this reading deficiency, no students with mental retardation could be included in her 6th grade science class, and only some of the students with learning disabilities could be included, if they could read at a level high enough to succeed (by reading the text, reading assignments, reading tests, and so forth).

This teacher was, of course, absolutely correct. Inclusion cannot succeed in her classroom. Students with disabilities in her science class will fail if they cannot read the material. This failure will frustrate many, if not most of these students, and some will begin to act out. They will also very likely fail to learn much in her class and are probably better off in another setting—perhaps a separate special education classroom. But does this mean that inclusion *cannot* work in a 6th grade science class for students who do not read on a 6th grade level? Of course not. What is critical to recognize from this example is that inclusion did not work in this 6th grade teacher's classroom because she made certain decisions, based on her assumptions about teaching and learning, and these decisions prevented many students from succeeding. This teacher stated that she did what she thought was in the best interests of her children: held all her students to the same high standards; wanted all her students to master the curriculum; expected all students to master the curriculum in the same way (mostly by reading the material); and tested all her students in the same way to ensure that they were making progress. She was adamant that what she was doing was "fair" for her students—fair meant doing the same thing for every student— and that this approach would help them become successful in life.

This teacher's perspective on teaching and learning is not unusual. Indeed, teachers in schools where we have worked to develop inclusive schools are faced with many pressures, primarily related to school accreditation, state-mandated tests of achievement, and local curriculum standards. These teachers are held accountable for ensuring that students meet certain curricular standards, and the teachers' perspectives toward teaching and learning are significantly influenced by these pressures. It must be recognized up front, as inclusive schools are being developed, that teachers and administrators are under much pressure to ensure that students meet certain curricular standards, and this important issue must be central to discussions of school change and inclusion.

With this background in mind, we often engage teams of teachers and administrators in an exploration of their views regarding teaching and learning using the "Discourses" included in Figure 4.2. Through these discussions, we hope to highlight beliefs that hinder or facilitate the development of inclusive schools. For example, consider Discourse A in Figure 4.2, which addresses the "Traditional Instruction" perspective on teaching and learning. The previously mentioned 6th grade science teacher would probably agree with this discourse and her beliefs would support the following (faulty) assumptions that emerge from these beliefs:

- Children should be ready to learn the curriculum of their grade level classroom.
- If a child fails to learn, the child is deficient.
- Services must be available in schools to "fix" children who are deficient.
- These services should be provided in separate settings until students catch up.
- Personnel with specialized skills are required for fixing students who are deficient.
- Children should be returned to the general education classroom when they are no longer deficient (that is, when they are fixed and can do the work everyone else does in the classroom).

—Figure 4.2—
DISCOURSES ON TEACHING AND LEARNING

Discourse A: Traditional Instruction
Children come to school with varying abilities, motivation, and life experiences. When these internal factors cause them to fail in school, it is the school district's responsibility to provide remedial, compensatory, or special services. Generating resources necessary to support these services requires identifying and labeling students as At-Risk, Chapter I, or Special Education. Specialists have developed tools and strategies to assess and plan for these students, often in separate settings, to meet their extraordinary needs. Specially trained personnel working in specially designed and delivered programs can provide the remediation and compensatory instruction that afford these students equitable educational opportunities (Burrello, Lashley, & Van Dyke, 1996, p. 33).

Discourse B: Inclusive Schools
All students attend the school to which they would normally go if they had no disability. Students with disabilities are distributed in their natural proportion at the school site in regular education programs that are age and grade appropriate. No student is denied placement at the school site on the basis of the severity of disability unless he or she is a danger to himself or herself or others. All students are in the regular classroom, unless specific circumstances cause educators to place them in other educational environments. Special education support services are primarily provided within the context of the regular education program in addition to other cooperative learning and peer support practices. Only in this way can students be assured of an equitable and appropriate education (Burrello, Lashley, & Van Dyke, 1996, p. 33).

- Fairness means requiring the same thing from every student in a general education classroom.

Inclusion will not and cannot work as long as teachers and administrators in a school subscribe to Discourse A and the assumptions that emerge from this discourse. More than anything else, successful inclusive schools require that teachers and administrators begin to think differently concerning what students are like, what a school should be like, and how an education should be delivered in a school. In a nutshell, "fair" must be defined as providing every student with what he or she needs rather than providing the same thing for every student. Moreover, students are identified with disabilities because they could not master the general education curriculum (at least in the area of the student's disability) in the same way that most other students master the curriculum. Thus, placing these students back into a general education classroom with the same expectations will ensure that the students fail once more.

To further address this issue, consider Discourse B in Figure 4.2, which is more in keeping with inclusive schools. The 6th grade science teacher previously quoted obviously would not agree with much of this discourse and would also likely disagree with the assumptions that emerge from this discourse:

- Students are "ready" to learn curriculum material at different times.
- Some students learn curricular material more quickly than others.
- Classroom curriculum, instruction, and so forth should be adapted to meet the needs of students.
- Services must be provided to support students and their teachers to ensure that the needs of a diverse range of students are met in general education classrooms.
- Support services should be provided, in most instances, in general education classrooms.
- Good teaching is good teaching is good teaching. Some students require more "good teaching" than other students. There are no specialized methods that work for one group of students and not for another.

- Children should be removed from a diverse, highly supportive general education classroom only when it is determined that their needs are so intense or challenging that they cannot be met in the general education classroom.
- Fairness means providing different curricula, instructions, expectations, and testing for students, depending on what the student needs to progress academically and socially.

These assumptions provide the foundation for developing successful inclusive school programs. Once teachers buy into Discourse B and its related assumptions, a solid foundation for developing inclusive schools has been laid. These assumptions require that teachers begin to think differently about learning, teaching, and schooling. As teachers and administrators are discussing these discourses, we use an exercise to help them focus on the students in their school and the needs of these students. To do so, they think about the students who are currently in their school and determine what the long-term goals for these students should be. The facilitators typically ask, "What would you like your students to be like long after they have left your classroom and school? What terms or phrases would you use to describe the qualities you would like to see in your students?" Figure 4.3 provides an example of the responses from four school-based teams we worked with in a large group as they considered this question. What is noteworthy about these responses is that most of the goals have little to do with academics. Most are personal goals (e.g., be happy, take responsibility for self) or societal goals (e.g., be a productive member of society) rather than academic goals. We encourage team members to consider the goals they hold for students as they discuss and reflect upon the previous "discourses" as well as when they develop the plans for their inclusive school.

The preceding discourses and activities encourage teams from schools to begin examining the learning and social communities of the school, and this examination does not end with these activities but continues as plans for the inclusive school are developed and implemented. We encourage teachers and administrators to get into the habit of reflecting on their beliefs concerning teaching and learn-

—Figure 4.3—
STUDENT LONG-TERM GOALS

Think about the students you have now. What are your long-term goals for these students? What would you like them to be like long after they have left your classroom and school?

Societal Goals
– Is a productive member of society
– Is a wise consumer
– Is tolerant of others
– Is an active participant in the community
– Takes on social/civic responsibility
– Is not on welfare or in the court news
– Is sexually responsible
– Makes positive social judgments
– Has self-control
– Demonstrates good social skills
– Is a good parent
– Cares about work

Academic Goals
– Is a good writer and verbal communicator
– Reads widely
– Counts money
– Is a lifelong learner
– Is an information seeker

Relationship Goals
– Has quality relationships
– Gets along with coworkers
– Cares about people
– Is accountable

Problem Solving
– Is a real-life problem solver
– Is a thinker
– Takes initiative
– Is resourceful

Personal Goals
– Accepts responsibility for choices
– Is a good role model
– Is respectful
– Is kind
– Is flexible
– Makes intelligent choices
– Plans ahead
– Is happy
– Is confident
– Finds creative niche
– Practices good health habits
– Is self-motivated
– Has good self-esteem
– Feels successful
– Is self-sacrificing
– Is joyful
– Is responsible for self—doesn't blame others
– Knows how to "play the game of life"
– Perseveres
– Is compassionate
– Is inquiring—has a bright and shiny mind
– Is self-fulfilled

Independent
– Is self-sufficient
– Is independent
– Has strength of character to change a situation
– Takes the next step

ing and on how they can change their school to ensure that *all* students are fully engaged members of the learning and social communities of the school. For example, Chapters 6 and 7 emphasize the need for teachers to continue to reflect on student learning and how students fit into the academic and social communities of the classroom. This critical reflection helps to ensure that teachers and administrators will think of the inclusive school as a work in progress, continually in need of examination and improvement. These activities also ensure that all teachers and administrators are engaged in the discussion regarding the particulars of the inclusive school that will be developed and implemented in their school.

Teacher Support for Inclusion

One final issue about teacher beliefs about inclusion merits discussion. We were discussing inclusion with an elementary principal from a school with a successful inclusion program, when he said,

EXAMPLE

> I don't have any teachers with a "bad attitude" toward inclusion. Don't get me wrong, not everybody strongly supports inclusion . . . but the issue seems to be helping teachers understand what inclusion is, how it works, how students benefit from it. How could any teacher not support inclusion if they really understood what it's all about? I think it's an issue of what teachers believe and understand about inclusion. Will it work for students? Can they handle it in their classrooms? Will it affect students who are not labeled? Every teacher is willing to teach every student, if they feel the student will benefit and they [the teacher] can handle their classroom. That's what teaching is all about!

We strongly agree with this principal's perspective. All too often, teacher resistance to inclusion is characterized as a bad attitude toward teaching students with disabilities. We have rarely seen a teacher who was unwilling to teach a student with a disability under any circumstances. Most often, resistance to teaching students relates to fears that the teacher has about his or her competence in meeting the needs of the students or questions about the benefits of inclusion for students with and without disabilities. These are reasonable concerns that any good teacher should have—concerns that should be addressed as inclusive programs are being developed and implemented. It is critical that teachers' questions and concerns about inclusion not be ascribed to a bad attitude or teacher resistance to inclusion. Most teachers—any good teacher—will support inclusion, *if* they understand what inclusion is, are involved in decision making regarding inclusion, and are provided reasonable support as they develop and implement an inclusive program.

Logistical Issues in Developing Inclusive Classrooms

EXAMPLE

One of the authors was visiting an elementary school that had recently implemented an inclusive program. The general education teacher had just completed taking roll and handling the daily chores necessary to get the day off to a good start. As reading was beginning, the special education teacher entered the classroom. She went to a table in the back of the room, and four students with disabilities joined her. The general education teacher gathered the remaining 20 students in the front of the room. The special education teacher began working on a phonics lesson with "her" students, while the general education teacher was discussing a book she had been reading to the rest of the class for the past week. This approach to reading was routinely used in this 3rd grade classroom.

We have been in many other settings much like this 3rd grade classroom, which purport to be inclusive, yet seem to continue to segregate and stigmatize students with disabilities. In the preceding example, we would ask why the teachers had bothered moving the resource class into the general education classroom. Is it not likely that the students with disabilities will be even more stigmatized by having their separate instruction in the general education classroom? The purpose of inclusion must not be simply to replicate special education services in the general education classroom, although this happens all too often. Indeed, we would contend that inclusive classrooms are successful only to the extent that they can accommodate most of the needs of students with disabilities in ways that are a natural and unobtrusive part of the school day. Put another way, the ultimate goal of inclusion is to make an increasingly wider range of differences ordinary in a general education classroom. This chapter describes four crucial issues to address to meet this goal: (1) create inclusive classrooms where a broad range of student differences are accommodated as an ordinary part of the school day; (2) provide supports for students that are a natural and unobtrusive part of the ongoing classroom routine; (3) ensure that the "rhythm" of the school day for students with disabilities is as typical as possible; and (4) ensure that students with disabilities are active participants in the academic and social communities of the classroom.

Making Differences Ordinary

EXAMPLE

One of the authors attended a case conference for a 7-year-old student who was having difficulty in her 2nd grade classroom. Rosa was identified as mildly mentally retarded. Her teacher stated that Rosa always worked hard on academic tasks and was very attentive in class. Rosa's mother worked with her on homework every evening, sometimes for several hours, in an attempt to help Rosa meet her teacher's expectations and succeed in 2nd grade.

Rosa's teacher was concerned that Rosa could not successfully complete all the work that other children in her classroom could and that Rosa could not successfully participate in many classroom activities because of her limited academic skills. The teacher went on to suggest that Rosa would be more successful in a 1st grade classroom or in a separate special education class, where classwork could be provided that was "on her level."

After the case conference meeting ended, Rosa's mother noted that Rosa had none of the problems that her 2nd grade teacher

—continued—

EXAMPLE

—continued—

described when she was in 1st grade and that the demands for completing homework were much more reasonable during the previous year. The author then sought out Rosa's teacher from her previous year, to find out what happened between 1st and 2nd grade. Rosa's 1st grade teacher described Rosa much as the 2nd grade teacher described her. However, in contrast to the 2nd grade teacher, the 1st grade teacher said that Rosa participated in most of the activities in her classroom and made significant academic progress during her year in 1st grade.

In any classroom, a range of academic and social behaviors exists that are considered ordinary, typical, and acceptable. As every teacher and administrator knows, this range of behaviors is quite broad in some classes and very narrow (or at least not as broad) in others. Some teachers arrange their classes so they can tolerate and support a broad range of differences among students. For example, in classes where a broad range of differences are supported, students reading at a range of grade levels are supported and feel that they are part of the learning community in the classroom—they successfully participate in most classroom activities, and student outcomes are evaluated so that *all* students have a reasonable chance for success. Still other students, who have difficulty getting along with others in the classroom, are supported and made to feel that they are part of the social community of the classroom. In these classes, the behavior of these students and teacher responses to these behaviors are viewed as part of the "ordinary" activities of the classroom.

In contrast to the response these students would receive in this classroom, in other classes these same students would be viewed as outside the range of tolerance and support of the teacher. Their low reading level would cause them to be unable to successfully participate in many classroom activities, and their subsequent performance on tests would lead to failure and frustration. Further, their inability to get along with peers would lead to isolation and rejection in the classroom. These students would then feel that they were not a part of either the learning or the social community of the classroom.

We have come to view classrooms from the perspective of a "circle of tolerance." Students whose behaviors fall within this circle are viewed as "normal" and the responses to their academic and social behaviors are perceived to be "ordinary" responses of the teacher to an acceptable range of student differences. In contrast, students who fall outside this circle of tolerance are viewed as "abnormal" and require specialized services that are not an ordinary part of the general education classroom. We have yet to find a teacher or classroom that could tolerate the full range of academic achievement and student behaviors that exist in schools; some students continue to need to be separated from peers for their own good as well as for the benefit of their peers. However, we also have never worked with a teacher who could not expand his or her circle of tolerance to make a broader range of differences ordinary. If inclusion is to be successful, the goal of change within classrooms must be to expand the circle of tolerance in a classroom, so that a broader range of behaviors is tolerated and provided for through supports that are an ordinary part of the classroom; thus, a broader range of student differences becomes ordinary (Biklen, 1989) in the general education classroom.

Making Classroom Supports Natural and Unobtrusive

There are two primary alternatives for increasing the range of academic and social behaviors that can be accommodated in a general education classroom. The first option is to add resources to the classroom. This may be done in a number of ways, including adding a special education teacher for part of the school day as a collaborator (e.g., coteacher) with the general education teacher, providing the classroom teacher with an instructional assistant, or reducing class size (thereby giving the teacher more time to work with each student). A second option for increasing the circle of tolerance is to change the classroom, for example, by altering what students are expected to learn and how they are taught. Regardless of which options are chosen for making a wider range of differences ordinary in the general education classroom, much evidence indicates that the supports that work best and continue to be used over time are those that fit naturally into the ebb and flow of the general education classroom (Gersten, Vaughn, Deshler, & Schiller, 1997; Giangreco, Dennis, Cloninger, Edelman, & Schattman, 1993).

Two general principles are useful in guiding the selection of alternatives being considered to increase the circle of tolerance of the general education classroom:

1. Use the most natural supports for the classroom setting.
2. Use the least intrusive supports that are effective.

These principles are adapted from work that has been done related to supported employment (Szymanski & Parker, 1989).

To illustrate the importance of considering these principles, let's examine teacher reactions when resources are added to the general education classroom as part of an inclusive program. Several authors have noted difficulties that may arise when a special education teacher assumes the role of coteacher or an instructional assistant is added to the classroom (Ferguson, Meyer, Jeanchild, Juniper, & Zingo, 1992; Giangreco, Dennis, Cloninger, Edelman, & Schattman, 1993; Giangreco, Edelman, & Dennis, 1991). For example, Giangreco and colleagues (1993) interviewed classroom teachers who received assistance in supporting students with substantial needs in their classrooms. Several of these teachers noted that they received some help that they could do without. "'Help' to address goals not identified or shared by teachers or referenced to the classroom program was not helpful. 'Help' that disrupted the classroom routine, as well as 'help' that was overly technical and specialized, also was identified as not helpful. Such 'help' was sometimes confusing to teachers or considered irrelevant" (p. 367). Giangreco and colleagues go on to note that these teachers were "involved in important work with their entire class and that anything that interfered with their mission was unacceptable. Most teachers indicated that the presence of a student with a disability did not create any more disruption than other students without disabilities. However, the presence of the specialists and other visitors who accompanied the students with disabilities did" (p. 367).

Ferguson (1995) has noted that these difficulties not only have a negative effect on the academic progress that students make in the classroom but also may negatively influence the social acceptance of students with disabilities and contribute to the *dependence* of these students on adults in the classroom. She describes observing students with disabilities who were "Velcroed" to "clipboard-bearing adults" as well as those who were "sitting apart in classrooms with an adult hovering over them showing them how to use books and papers unlike any others in class" (p. 284). She notes that these students "seemed *in*, but not *of* the class" (p. 284). She goes on to note that "these students were caught inside a bubble that teachers didn't seem to notice but that nonetheless succeeded in keeping other students and teachers at a distance" (p. 284). Thus, these students were prevented from developing meaningful relationships with other students in the classrooms (and at times with the classroom teacher or other adults) and became far too dependent on one adult in the classroom.

Similar difficulties may occur when general education classrooms are changed by altering what students are expected to learn and how they are taught. For example, Giangreco and colleagues (1993) noted that classroom teachers favored the use of "typical activities, materials, and approaches over special ones" (p. 367). While specialists did not always agree with the classroom teachers in this regard, one teacher noted that the specialists "get so specialized that they overlook the simple things" (p. 367). They go on to note that "teachers recognized that some 'special' approaches were helpful and necessary, while others are potentially unnecessary and stigmatizing" (p. 368). Giangreco and colleagues conclude by stating that "when specialists attempted to transplant traditional special education practices into general education environments, this was neither welcomed nor considered helpful by general education teachers" (p. 371). This resulted in several teachers' viewing the role of the specialist as a barrier to inclusion rather than as facilitative.

A final reason for ensuring that supports in the general education classroom are natural and unobtrusive is that teachers will continue to use supports that meet these criteria and will quickly discontinue using supports that are obtrusive and that don't fit the ebb and flow of the general education classroom (Gersten, Vaughn, Deshler, & Schiller, 1997). Gersten and colleagues have suggested, among other things, that for classroom supports to be sustained over time, they must

- Fit the details of day-to-day classroom instruction.
- Be perceived by teachers as being effective for typical students as well as for students with disabilities.
- Enhance the teacher's current repertoire of instructional methods.

It is important to note that we are not suggesting that changes should not occur in the daily routine of the general education classroom. On the contrary, successful inclusive classrooms cannot be developed without such changes. What is being suggested is that special education cannot simply be replicated in the general education classroom, any more than general education classrooms can remain the same and successfully support students with disabilities. We agree with Ferguson (1995), who has stated that "in trying to change everything, inclusion all too often seems to be leaving everything the same. But in a new place" (p. 284). Pugach (1995) suggests that this lack of change is influenced by the perspective that is taken by some special educators that "inclusion, like its predecessor, mainstreaming, is essentially a function of what the field of special education is already doing . . . the answer to the challenge of inclusion lies only in what special education already knows how to do relative to the status quo in general education" (p. 218). This perspective obviously does not recognize the changes that need to occur in both general and special education if successful inclusive classrooms are to be developed.

In sum, when students fall outside a teacher's range of tolerance, supports must be provided that fit into the ongoing activities of the classroom as naturally and unobtrusively as possible, so that they are not viewed as simply importing special education services into the general education classroom. Indeed, Pugach (1995) has noted that, in the future, what counts as "special" may not always stand out in inclusive classrooms. "We might expect that at some point or another, each student might need to spend time in a small group to get . . . assistance . . . [and] that spending such time is a commonplace of the classroom and does not endanger a student's full and rightful membership in the community of learners" (p. 220). In short, general education classrooms are transformed into places where differences becomes ordinary.

Typical Rhythm of the Day for Students with Disabilities

One of the hallmarks of a good inclusive school program is that daily schedules and classroom activities for students with disabilities are as similar as possible to the daily schedules and classroom activities of students without disabilities. Thus, the "rhythm of the day" (Schwartz, 1991) for students with disabilities resembles that of the school day of other students in the school.

EXAMPLE

One of the authors was sitting in on a case conference that had gotten rather contentious. A 3rd grade girl, Hannah, was the point of contention for the participants. Hannah was a lovely, friendly student who had many friends in the school. Her teachers all described her as well-adjusted, friendly, and hard-working. As the room filled, there were 14 participants, including the school principal, parents, parent advocates, school psychologist, the speech/language therapist, the physical therapist, the special education teacher, three general education teachers, and others not identified. At the beginning of the meeting, I asked if everyone would explain why they were attending the meeting, to gain a better understanding of the interest all of these professionals had in a 3rd grade girl who had Down's syndrome and an IQ in the range of moderate mental retardation. As the responses went around the table, I counted the number of different professionals who

—continued—

—continued—

provided services for Hannah. As well as could be discerned, Hannah left her 3rd grade classroom for education or therapy of some sort at least eight times a week. She left class, as did other 3rd grade students, for art, music, and physical education. In addition, her home-base 3rd grade teacher stated that Hannah could not do 3rd grade work, so she was sent to 1st grade for some subjects, 2nd grade for others, and a separate special education classroom for basic skills instruction in reading and arithmetic. In addition, she was pulled out of her general education classroom for speech therapy twice a week and physical therapy twice a week. I asked the assembled mass of professionals if this was a typical schedule for a 3rd grade student. They all agreed that it was not, although they all agreed that Hannah found her way to the various classes and therapy sessions with no problem. My immediate thought was that this was quite an accomplishment for *any* 3rd grade student.

Schedules such as Hannah's are not atypical for students with disabilities who are taught in traditional, pull-out special education programs—especially for students with more substantial needs. Fragmented school days present many disadvantages, including the following:

• Moving to separate classes disrupts the student's routine and the routine of the general education classroom. Furthermore, the student will likely come and go during the middle of classroom activities and often will miss important academic content from the general education classroom.

• It's difficult for the student to make friends, especially when the student goes to more than one general education classroom and is pulled out at various times during the school day to go to special education and various therapy sessions.

• Instructional time is limited. Much time is lost as the student travels from one classroom to another, and it takes several minutes in each class to begin and end activities.

• Students must learn the rules of several different classrooms, making it difficult to learn appropriate behaviors for each setting. This problem becomes especially acute for students with behavior problems.

• Leaving the general education classroom may often stigmatize students. They are viewed as odd because they don't remain in the general education classroom during important instruction times.

• A fragmented schedule makes learning difficult for the student and violates almost every tenet of effective instruction.

If the rhythm of the day for students with disabilities is much like that of other students, they avoid many of these problems and have the potential for a much improved educational experience. Not only should a student's daily schedule reflect the rhythm of the day of other students, but the activities that students with disabilities engage in should be as typical or routine as possible, for reasons similar to those noted above.

EXAMPLE

In an inclusive 4th grade classroom, a classroom teacher and a teacher of students with disabilities were teaming to teach mathematics. As the class was reviewing mathematics problems before a test, the teacher of students with disabilities was going over the material with the class, while the classroom teacher was moving around the room to respond to questions and keep students on task. At the end of the review session, the teacher of students with disabilities asked all the students if they would like to have the test read to them. Approximately half the students in the class (including students with disabilities and students who were not thus labeled) raised their hands and subsequently left the classroom to have the test read, while the other students remained in the general education classroom to complete the test (McLeskey & Waldron, 1996, p. 152).

Two factors stand out regarding the rhythm of the day of the students in this 4th grade class. First, the two teachers shared roles, so that both worked with typical students as well as students with difficulties. Thus, neither was readily identifiable as a "special" teacher; both were just teachers. Second, all students—not just students with disabilities—were given the option of having the test read to them or remaining in the classroom for a more traditional test administration. Thus, although some students were "pulled out" of the classroom, the rhythm of the day for all of these students was similar (McLeskey & Waldron, 1996).

In sum, ensuring that the rhythm of the day for students with disabilities is similar to that of other students and that the supports provided to students with disabilities are as natural and unobtrusive as possible are critical considerations in developing inclusive classrooms. These considerations help to ensure that "difference becomes ordinary" in the general education classroom and that students with disabilities become part of the learning and social community of the classroom.

All Students as Part of the Learning and Social Classroom Communities

After completing a three-year research project related to the study of inclusive school programs, Ferguson (1995) came to a troubling realization. She noted that even when students with disabilities were assigned to general education classroom full-time,

> . . . their participation often fell short of the kind of social and learning membership that most proponents of inclusion envision. . . . Even to casual observers, some students seemed set apart—immediately recognizable as different—not so much because of any particular impairment or disability but because of what they were doing, with whom, and how (p. 284).

Ferguson (1995) concluded that a significant factor contributing to this lack of membership in the classroom was the fact that many of the teachers' (both general and special education) assumptions about students and learning remained unchallenged and unchanged. These included the following:

• "Inclusion" students were viewed as "irregular," even though they were in "regular" classes full-time.

- These students needed specialized "stuff" that could not be provided by the classroom teacher.
- The special educator was the officially designated provider of the specialized stuff.

These assumptions reflect a fundamental problem with many inclusion programs: that special education is simply moved into general education classrooms, without questioning what students with disabilities are taught, how they are taught, and by whom they are taught. These assumptions must be questioned and rejected if successful inclusion programs are to be developed and implemented.

An underlying assumption of successful inclusive programs is that all children will be included in the learning and social communities of the school and that classrooms in these schools will be so accepting of diversity that no one will be left out from the very beginning (Stainback, Stainback, & Jackson, 1992). The challenge to make general education classes places where a more diverse range of students can become part of the learning and social community is a more difficult task than many proponents of inclusion realized (Ferguson, 1995). There seems little doubt that neither general nor special education teachers alone have the knowledge and skills to achieve this goal, but rather that meaningful change will require that these educators collaborate "to reinvent schools to be more accommodating to all dimensions of human diversity" (Ferguson, 1995, p. 285). To achieve the goal of reinventing services that better meet the needs of all students, Ferguson suggests a logical approach that seems very useful. This approach begins "with the majority perspective and build[s] the tools and strategies for achieving inclusion from the center out rather than from the most exceptional child in" (p. 284). Based on this perspective, general and special educators collaborate to "invent the next generation of inclusive classrooms—and to go on generating knowledge that will facilitate the goal of inclusion in the long run" (Pugach, 1995, p. 218).

This approach to changing classrooms would suggest that teachers who are collaborating to make a classroom more accommodating of diversity begin with the curriculum, instruction, and organization of the general education classroom, then build in the tools and strategies for making all students part of the learning and social community of the classroom. A good beginning point for this discussion is to question what is taught in the general education classroom and how it is taught. Ferguson (1995) suggests that such a discussion address three types of shifts in general education classrooms that would make them more accommodating of student diversity:

- A shift away from organizing schools and classrooms based on ability or skill levels and toward schools that are structured to accommodate student diversity and the many different ways of organizing students for learning.
- A shift away from the teacher as disseminator of knowledge that students must retain "toward approaches that emphasize the role of the learner in creating knowledge, competence, and the ability to pursue further learning" (p. 287).
- A shift away from the view that the role of schools is to provide services for students to one of providing supports for learning. Thus, students are supported in their efforts to become active members of the learning community of the classroom.

A discussion of these issues provides a good beginning for reinventing the general education classroom as a learning and social community for a broad range of student needs. There is a broad range of options that teachers should consider in making the general education classroom more accommodating. (See Chapters 6 and 7 for a review of several of these options.) There is no formula for this process—far from it, successful inclusive classrooms are dynamic and ever-changing, as the needs of students, the content being covered, and available resources change. However, ensuring that "difference is ordinary" in a classroom, that supports provided students with disabilities are as natural and unobtrusive as possible, and that the rhythm of the day of students with disabilities is as much like that of other students as possible provides a sound foundation for building inclusive classrooms and schools in which students with disabilities are active participants in the learning and social communities.

Addressing Students' Academic Needs in Inclusive Classrooms

Perhaps the greatest challenge faced by teachers when inclusive programs are developed is addressing the wide range of academic needs that students bring into classrooms. Unfortunately, all too often schools are ill-prepared when students fail to learn using the typical methods in the general education classroom. Consider the following example.

Chuck is a bright, engaging 7-year-old who is repeating the 1st grade. During his first year in the 1st grade, Chuck was in a classroom that emphasized a "whole-language" approach to reading instruction. Throughout the school year, Chuck was highly motivated and cooperated with his teacher and parents as they had him read predictable books, write in a journal, and complete a variety of other activities in an attempt to help him learn to read. Midway through the school year, as it became apparent to Chuck's parents that he was not learning to read, they met with his teacher and the school principal on repeated occasions in an attempt to arrange an alternative method of reading instruction. It seemed clear to the parents that the whole-language method was not working. While the principal and teacher agreed that the whole-language method was not working for Chuck, they stated that this was the only method that was available in their school and that they did not have the funds to provide alternatives. The parents

—continued—

—continued—

noted that several other students in Chuck's class also were failing to progress in reading. At the end of his first year in 1st grade, Chuck was reading at a pre-primer level. The school principal met with Chuck's parents on the last day of school, expressed her frustration that the school did not do a better job with Chuck, and described her plan to offer more alternative approaches to reading instruction during the coming school year.

During his second year of 1st grade, Chuck moved to a school in another state. His teacher in this school used a more traditional approach to reading, built around a basal reading series. At the end of the first grading period, the teacher gave Chuck a very low grade in reading but noted that he was a very "nice boy to work with" and "worked very hard." By November, Chuck was still not making appreciable progress in learning to read. In a meeting to share this information, Chuck's parents were told that the basal series was the only reading method available in the general education classroom and that Chuck would have to be "pulled out" to receive alternative instruction as part of the school's Title I program. The principal further noted that the basal series was working for most other students in Chuck's class.

Chuck soon was pulled out of his reading/language arts instruction for 30 minutes each morning. During this time, he was taught, along with a small group of other students, using a highly structured, scripted (direct instruction) reading program. After three months in this program, the principal and teachers arranged a meeting with Chuck's parents, shared evaluative information, and stated that Chuck was making little progress in the Title I program. The principal noted that they were "baffled" regarding what to do with Chuck. She further noted that the only alternative available through the school was to offer Chuck instruction in the Title I program for an additional 30 minutes a day. When asked about other alternatives, the principal suggested that the Reading Recovery program might be a good option for Chuck but that his parents would have to arrange for this support after school.

Obviously, neither of the schools Chuck attended had well-developed inclusive programs. All students were expected to progress through a "set" reading instructional program in the general education classroom, and when students failed to progress, the difficulty was viewed as a problem with the student, not with the reading method or classroom organization. This chapter reviews methods that can be used to offer Chuck a better chance to succeed. More specifically, it reviews changes that may be made in the general education classroom to accommodate diversity and "make difference ordinary." Initially, methods are addressed that can be used to change the general education curriculum to accommodate diversity. This is followed by a review of methods that can be used to change the organization and delivery of instruction. Additional information regarding resources that may be useful for teachers as they address students' academic needs in inclusive classrooms is provided in the appendix.

Accommodating Diversity

There is some disagreement in the professional literature, as well as in practice, about the extent to which the general education curriculum should be changed to accommodate diversity. Some suggest that a modest approach involving curricular adaptations can be used to achieve this goal (Vaughn, Bos, & Schumm, 2000; Zigmond & Baker, 1997); others strongly state that the curriculum must be dramatically changed to accommodate diverse student needs (Ferguson, 1995; Pugach & Warger, 1996; Udvari-Solner & Thousand, 1996). We have found that both alternatives are being successfully used in schools and will address them in the following sections.

Adapting the General Education Curriculum

It is important to recognize that students with disabilities cannot learn everything that other students learn, in the same way that other students learn in the area of their disability. For example, a middle school student with a learning disability in the area of reading will not be able to learn science content as readily as other students in her class by reading the material. Similarly, a middle school student who is moderately mentally retarded will not be able to learn information in science at as high a conceptual level as most of his grade-level peers.

Thus, if inclusion is to be successful and students with disabilities are to be part of the classroom learning community, there must be a fundamental change in the general education classroom so it is accepted that not all students will learn the same things, in the same way, at the same time. Thus, adaptations of the general education curriculum are necessary as well as alterations in what is expected of students and how progress is evaluated.

Vaughn, Bos, and Schumm (2000) take the perspective that much of the work in adapting instruction for a diverse range of students should be addressed in planning instruction for the entire classroom. They provide extensive information regarding planning for the school year as well as for units and lessons. We will take a brief look at their approach for unit and lesson planning, a curricular adaptation that many schools have found useful.

Vaughn and colleagues (2000) build their approach to planning on a concept called Degrees of Learning. The basic premise underlying this concept is that "although all students are capable of learning, not all students will learn all the content covered" (p. 47). They go on to provide an example of unit planning that applies the Degrees of Learning concept, using earth science content related to weathering and erosion. To guide decision making regarding this content, Vaughn and colleagues (2000) recommend that teachers use a Unit Planning Form (see Figure 6.1). The base of the planning pyramid in Figure 6.1 represents content that is essential for *all* students to learn, such as the basic components of the earth's surface. The middle part of the pyramid is information that is important for *most* but not all students to learn, such as the basic types of rocks. The top of the pyramid represents information that the teacher expects only a few students to learn, students who "have an added interest in and desire to learn more about the subject" (p. 48). Information at the top includes how the earth looked during the Ice Age and geographic examples of slow and fast changes. As Figure

—Figure 6.1—
SAMPLE UNIT PLAN

UNIT PLANNING FORM

What *some* students will learn.	• *How Earth looked during the Ice Age* • *Disasters caused by sudden changes* • *Geographic examples of slow and fast changes*	Date: _Sept. 1–30_____ Class Period: __1:30–2:30___ Unit Title: _Weathering and Erosion_____ Materials/Resources: _Guest speaker on volcanoes_____ _Video: erosion and weathering_____ _Rock samples_____ _Library books: disasters, volcanoes, etc._____ _Colored transparencies for lectures_____
What *most* students will learn.	• *Compare and contrast weathering and erosion* • *How humans cause physical and chemical weathering* • *Basic types of rocks*	Instructional Strategies/Adaptations: _Experiments!_____ _Concept maps_____ _Cooperative learning groups to learn material_ __in textbook_____ _Audiotape of chapter_____ _Study buddies to prepare for quizzes and tests_ Evaluation/Products: _Weekly quiz_____
What *all* students should learn.	• *Basic components of Earth's surface* • *Forces that change crust are weathering and erosion*	_Unit test_____ _Learning logs (daily record of "What I learned")_ _Vocabulary flash_____

Source: Vaughn, S., Bos, C. S., & Schumm, J. S. (2000). *Teaching Exceptional, Diverse, and At-Risk Students in the General Education Classroom* (2nd ed.) (p. 52). Boston: Allyn & Bacon. Copyright © 2000 by Allyn & Bacon. Reprinted by permission.

6.1 illustrates, in addition to planning what students will learn, Vaughn and colleagues (2000) recommend that the teacher determine the materials and resources that will be used to teach the unit, instructional strategies and adaptations that will be used, and how the content will be evaluated.

After unit planning is complete, Vaughn and colleagues (2000) recommend that a similar procedure be used to plan individual lessons. For example, if a teacher were planning an individual lesson related to the earth's surface, the teacher might determine that *all* students need to know that the earth has three layers and that the outer layer is where we live. In addition, *most* students should learn how rocks are formed and that the crust is made up of three types of rocks. Finally, *some* students would learn the three types of rocks.

While many advantages are associated with the use of this approach to instructional planning, Vaughn and colleagues (2000) offer the following cautions when this approach is used:

• All students should have the opportunity to be exposed to the same information, although how the information is presented may vary, depending on the student's needs.

• All students should "have equal access to information representing all levels of the pyramid" (p. 49).

• Assignments to particular levels of the pyramid should not be made based on students' ability. Students who learn at the higher levels of the pyramid should do so based on their interests, prior knowledge, or personal experiences.

• Instruction and related activities addressing the content at the bottom of the pyramid should not be less stimulating (e.g., worksheets, dittos) than instruction and activities at the other levels, "nor should the upper levels be viewed as the place for creative, fun activities" (p. 49).

(For additional information regarding curricular planning, see Vaughn and colleagues, 2000.)

A second resource for curricular adaptation that many teachers have found useful is provided by Deschenes, Ebeling, and Sprague (1994), who describe a systematic approach to planning classroom instruction and adapting to individual student needs. These authors suggest that teachers often use one of nine types of adaptations for students with disabilities in inclusive classrooms (see Figure 6.2). These adaptations are designed to provide all students with the opportunity to participate to the maximum extent possible in typical activities of the classroom. Deschenes and colleagues provide an extensive description of this adaptation process, along with examples from elementary and secondary classrooms. In addition to this information, they provide suggestions for a range of accommodations that can be made in the inclusive classroom to ensure that students with disabilities participate fully as members of the learning

—Figure 6.2— NINE TYPES OF INSTRUCTIONAL ADAPTATIONS		
Adaptation	**Definition**	**Example**
Size	Adapt the number of items that the learner is expected to learn or complete	Reduce the number of spelling items the learner must complete
Time	Adapt the time allocated for learning, task completion, or testing	Individualize a time line for completing a task
Level of Support	Increase the amount of personal assistance with a specific learner	Assign peer buddies
Input	Adapt the way instruction is delivered	Use more concrete examples
Difficulty	Adapt the skill level, problem type, or rules	Allow use of calculator to figure math problems
Output	Adapt how the student responds to instruction	Instead of written responses, allow verbal response
Participation	Adapt the extent to which a learner is actively involved in a task	Ask a student to sit with a peer and listen to the peer read vocabulary words and definitions
Alternate Goals	Adapt the goals or outcome while using the same material	Ask one student to learn the names of states, while others learn this information as well as state capitals
Substitute Curriculum	Provide different instruction and materials to meet a student's individual goals	During a language test one student is learning computer skills in the computer lab

Source: Adapted from Deschenes, C., Ebeling, D., & Sprague, J. (1994). *Adapting Curriculum & Instruction in Inclusive Classrooms: A Teacher's Desk Reference* (p. 19). Bloomington, IN: Institute for the Study of Developmental Disabilities. Reprinted by permission.

community of the classroom. A summary of these suggestions is provided in Figure 6.3.

It is noteworthy that the approaches to adapting curriculum in the general education classroom that are provided by both Vaughn and

---

−Figure 6.3−
Strategies for Adapting Curriculum and Instruction

Adapting Classroom Instruction
- Allow students to work in a pair or small group to complete assignments.
- Present information through a multi-sensory approach.
- Write key points on the board or overhead and read them aloud.
- Use samples of finished products as models.
- Provide clear, visually uncluttered handouts and worksheets.
- Provide several options for students to demonstrate knowledge (e.g., oral, artwork).
- Provide study guides that identify key vocabulary and concepts.
- Allow extra credit projects to bring up grades.
- Provide frequent positive feedback.
- Allow extra time in class or outside of class for work completion.

Adapting Written Assignments
- Reduce length and/or complexity of written assignments or allow more time for completion.
- Do not penalize students for errors in spelling, punctuation, and grammar.
- Allow students to have a photocopy or peer's class notes.
- Mark the number of items correct on papers instead of the wrong number.
- Do not return handwritten work to be copied over; the paper is often not improved, and frustration is increased.
- Provide credit for late assignments or partial completion.
- Simplify written directions by limiting words and numbering steps.
- Allow students to dictate answers to peers, tape recorders, parents, and others.
- Pair students for completion of written assignments.

Adapting Reading Assignments
- Provide stories and chapters on tape; ask for help from assistants, parents, peers, and others to make tapes.
- Allow students to work with peers on reading assignments.
- Recognize the value of listening comprehension; allow for partial participation.
- Ask parents to provide extra practice with reading.

Adapting Homework Assignments
- Communicate homework expectations to parents, and solicit input on modifications that need to be made for the student.
- Make arrangements for assignments to reach home with clear, concise directions and time lines.
- Reduce homework assignments.
- Allow homework papers to be typed by the student or dictated and recorded by someone else.
- Coordinate homework assignments with other teachers the student may have, to avoid overloading the student.
- Clarify the goals of homework for the student and make adaptations accordingly.

Adapting Tests, Quizzes, and Grades
- Provide students with the opportunity to have the test read orally.
- Reduce the number of items or simplify the terminology or concepts.
- Allow students to retake tests and give credit for improvement.
- Provide a menu of options for students to demonstrate knowledge other than or in addition to tests (e.g., projects, extra assignments).
- Allow students to take tests with classmates in pairs or small groups.
- Provide study guides with key concepts and vocabulary in advance of tests or quizzes.
- Create a modified grade scale or grade on a pass/fail basis.
- Provide information on the standard report card indicating that adaptations have been made.

Source: Adapted from Deschenes, C., Ebeling, D., & Sprague, J. (1994). *Adapting Curriculum & Instruction in Inclusive Classrooms: A Teacher's Desk Reference* (pp. 53–55). Bloomington, IN: Institute for the Study of Developmental Disabilities. Reprinted by permission.

colleagues (2000) and Deschenes and colleagues (1994) assume that the general education curriculum will remain essentially unchanged. Other professionals have suggested that if inclusion is to be successful, more fundamental changes in the general education curriculum must occur. This perspective is addressed in the next section of this chapter.

Transforming the General Education Curriculum

Some have suggested that, if inclusive classrooms are to include a wide range of students with disabilities as members of their learning and social communities, significant changes in the general education curriculum are required. Pugach (1995), for example, has stated that failing to question and change the general education curriculum results in an "additive" approach to school change, in which the basic assumptions underlying the general education classroom are unchallenged. These assumptions suggest that

- The curriculum of the general education classroom is acceptable.
- The role of special educators is to "soften the blow" of the curriculum by adapting it.
- Practices such as strategy instruction (Deshler, Ellis, & Lenz, 1996), classwide peer tutoring (Mathes, Fuchs, Fuchs, Hanley, & Sanders, 1994), and curriculum-based measurement (Tindal & Marston, 1990) provide an adequate buffer for the dilemmas posed by the standard curriculum paradigm and standard teaching practices (p. 216).

Pugach (1995) goes on to note that general education classrooms are thus "created from a stance of what we already know and are already comfortable with, built on an existing vision of what it means to teach and learn, and, specifically in terms of special education, what it means to support students who are having difficulty in school" (p. 216). Programs built upon these assumptions, according to Pugach, do "not seem powerful enough to recreate and restructure classrooms and schools such that inclusion can take place with confidence" (p. 216).

At the most basic level, Pugach (1995) and others (Poplin & Stone, 1992) are criticizing the reductionist or behavioral approach to learning and teaching upon which most traditional classroom practices are built. Underlying this approach to teaching and learning are the following assumptions (Nolan & Francis, 1992; Udvari-Solner & Thousand, 1996):

- Learning takes place only in a rigid hierarchical progression.
- Learning is the accumulation of fragments of information.
- Teachers transfer knowledge intact to students.
- Children must master lower-level skills and knowledge before mastering higher-level skills and knowledge.
- Classroom process focuses on how teachers and individual students interact.
- Skills transfer across subject areas.
- The goal of teaching is to change student behavior.

In contrast to this traditional, reductionist view of teaching and learning, which results in an additive model of curriculum and classroom change, Pugach (1995) suggests that a generative model of change would be much more likely to produce successful inclusive classrooms. This approach demands that the general education curriculum be redesigned, based upon the tenets that underlie much of the curriculum reform being undertaken in general education in the fields of literacy, mathematics, science, and social studies (Pugach & Warger, 1996). This curriculum reform movement rejects more traditional notions of teaching and learning and embraces a constructivist approach to learning and teaching. A constructivist model is built upon the following assumptions (Nolan & Francis, 1992; Udvari-Solner & Thousand, 1996):

- For learning to occur, learners must actively construct meaning.
- Learning is the creation of meaning that occurs when an individual makes connections, associations, and links between new and existing learning.
- Learning is not quantitative but rather is interpretive and requires social contexts of communities and communicative interchanges to develop.
- Learning is a cooperative, collaborative endeavor.
- The goal of teaching is to change students' cognitive structures.

―Figure 6.4―
COMPARING TRADITIONAL AND CONSTRUCTIVIST CLASSROOMS

Traditional Classrooms	Constructivist Classrooms
– Curriculum presented part to whole	– Curriculum presented whole to part
– Emphasis on basic skills	– Emphasis on big concepts
– Fixed curriculum	– Pursuit of student questions
– Use of textbooks and workbooks	– Use of primary sources of information
– Students viewed as blank slates	– Students viewed as active learners/thinkers
– Seek "correct" answers	– Seek students' point of view
– Assessment separate from learning	– Assessment and instruction interwoven
– Test knowledge of fixed content	– Student exhibitions and portfolios
– Students primarily work alone	– Students work primarily in groups

Source: Adapted from In Search of Understanding: The Case for Constructivist Classrooms (p. 17) by J. G. Brooks & M. Brooks. Alexandria, VA: Association for Supervision and Curriculum Development. Copyright © 1993 by ASCD. Reprinted by permission. All rights reserved.

Figure 6.4 provides a comparison of how these approaches to learning and teaching are reflected in different classroom practices (Brooks & Brooks, 1993). It is noteworthy that many of the changes that occur as classrooms move from a traditional to a constructivist perspective are (1) changes that many reformers are calling for as part of the current educational reform movement; (2) viewed by many as important changes to ensure successful inclusive classrooms (Pugach, 1995; Tomlinson, 1995; Udvari-Solner & Thousand, 1996); and (3) reflected in several of the approaches to curriculum and instruction currently being advocated for helping teachers support diversity in general education classrooms, including multi-age grouping, multicultural education, interdisciplinary or thematic curriculum, and cooperative learning (Udvari-Solner & Thousand, 1996). In a similar vein, Pugach and Warger (1996) have noted that the movement to reform the academic curriculum in general education has many rich possibilities for supporting special educators in their quest for worthwhile school experiences for students with disabilities, experiences that make difference ordinary for students with disabilities who are educated in general education classrooms. Some of these developments include the following:

- Covering less material, but covering it in more depth.
- Focusing on the meaning of what is learned rather than the facts and figures.
- Teaching as the facilitation of student learning.
- Linking ideas across subject matter.
- Constructing rather than receiving knowledge; beginning where the students are and building on their prior knowledge.
- Creating an authentic activity orientation for learning in which students work as part of a classroom community.
- Embedding the acquisition of basic skills into meaningful activities.
- Engaging students in cooperative work and problem solving.
- Closely aligning curriculum, instruction, and assessment (Pugach & Warger, 1996, p. 229).

Resources that provide further information regarding curricular changes in inclusive classrooms are described in the appendix.

Accommodating Diversity in the General Education Classroom

Scott, Vitale, and Masten (1998) have suggested that alternatives for accommodating diversity in inclusive general education classrooms include modifying instruction and varying instructional groupings. These authors note that instructional modifications may be either "typical" (e.g., concrete classroom demonstrations) or "substantial" (e.g., adjusting the pace to individual learners), while varying instructional groupings most often requires a substantial change in the classroom (e.g., using cooperative groups).

Modifying Instruction

As Tomlinson (1995) states, "At its most basic level, differentiating instruction means 'shaking up' what goes on in the classroom so that students have multiple options for taking in information, making sense of ideas, and expressing what they learn" (p. 3). Tomlinson goes on to note that differentiated instruction is *not* the "individual-ized instruction" that was in vogue in the 1970s, which attempted to provide something different for each of 25–30 students in the class-room, nor is it homogeneous grouping. In contrast to these ideas, effective differentiated instruction has the following qualities (Tomlinson, 1995):

- *It is proactive.* Teachers assume different learners have differ-ing needs and plan lessons and units to accommodate these needs.
- *It is more qualitative than quantitative.* Differentiating is not just giving students more or less work to do. Adjusting the quantity of work is less effective than adjusting the nature of the work to match student needs.
- *It provides multiple approaches to content* (what students learn), *process* (how students make sense of ideas and information), *and product* (how students demonstrate that they have learned).
- *It is student centered.* Classrooms thus operate on the premise that students learn more when learning experiences are engaging, relevant, and interesting. Furthermore, what a student learns will be built upon previous learning, and not all students possess the same understandings.
- *It is a blend of individual, small group, and whole-class instruc-tion.* Whole-group instruction is used to develop common under-standings and a sense of community, while small groups or individual work is used to address more particular student needs. Grouping is thus flexible and fluid.
- *It is "organic."* This assumes that teachers will constantly learn about how their students learn and adapt what they do in the class-room on the basis of what they learn. Thus, differentiated instruction is a dynamic process, as teachers monitor what and how students are learning and adapt the classroom as needed to better meet stu-dent needs.

Tomlinson (1995) goes on to note that differentiating instruction is not simply giving a "normal" assignment to most students and giv-ing "different" assignments to students who are struggling or those who are advanced. This approach tends to create a pecking order in the classroom, and students who are given remedial assignments may take it as a sign that they are inferior. In an effective differentiated classroom, many different things are happening, no one assignment defines "normal," and no one "sticks out." The teacher thinks and plans in terms of multiple avenues of learning for varied needs rather than in terms of "normal" and "different." Thus, the classroom is designed and instructional plans are made that provide students with a rich range of alternatives for learning and for demonstrating what they have learned (Tomlinson, 1995). See Figure 6.5 for a comparison of the qualities of traditional and differentiated classrooms (Tomlinson, 1999). This information illustrates how classrooms change to become more accommodating of student diversity. For resources containing more detailed information regarding differentiated classrooms, see the appendix.

Varying Instructional Groupings

Inclusion began, in large part, because of the lack of success achieved by students with disabilities when they were placed in ability groups and kept in these groups for long periods of time, with little opportunity to interact with students who were moving through academic content at a more rapid pace. Thus, inclusion is not intended to return students with disabilities to general education classrooms where they will be grouped with other students with similar instructional needs for most or all of the school day. It is important to also note that inclusion is not intended to prevent *any* grouping of students with disabilities into skills groups. As Vaughn, Bos, and Schumm (2000) have noted, research has not identified one "best" approach to grouping. Rather, many teachers have realized that a variety of grouping patterns is best for a classroom with a diverse range of students. Thus, different grouping patterns should be used for different purposes, including whole groups, same-ability small groups, mixed-ability small groups, and cooperative groups.

Vaughn and colleagues (2000) go on to suggest that flexible grouping patterns are needed for successful inclusive classrooms and that these grouping patterns should be built upon five principles (Unsworth, 1984):

—Figure 6.5—
COMPARING TRADITIONAL AND DIFFERENTIATED CLASSROOMS

Traditional Classrooms	Differentiated Classrooms
Student differences are masked or acted upon when problematic	Student differences are studied as a basis for planning
Assessment is most common at the end of learning to see "who got it"	Assessment is ongoing and used to understand how to make instruction more responsive to learner needs
A single definition of excellence exists	Excellence is defined in large measure by individual growth from a starting point
Whole-class instruction dominates	Many instructional arrangements are used
Coverage of texts and curriculum guides drives instruction	Student readiness, interest, and learning profile shape instruction
Single-option assignments are the norm	Multi-option assignments are frequently used
Time is relatively inflexible	Time is used flexibly in accordance with student needs
A single text prevails	Multiple materials are provided
The teacher directs student behavior	The teacher facilitates students' skills at becoming more self-reliant learners
The teacher solves problems	Students help other students and the teacher solve problems
The teacher provides whole-class standards for grading	Students work with the teacher to establish both whole-class and individual learning goals
A single form of assessment is used	Students are assessed in multiple ways

Source: Adapted from *The Differentiated Classroom: Responding to the Needs of All Learners* (p. 16) by C. A. Tomlinson. Alexandria, VA: Association for Supervision and Curriculum Development. Copyright © 1999 by ASCD. Reprinted by permission. All rights reserved.

- There should be no permanent groups.
- Periodically, groups should be created, modified, or disbanded, depending on student needs.
- At times there may be only one group, consisting of all students in the class.
- Depending on the activity and purpose of the group, the size of the group should vary from 2 or 3 to 9 or 10 students.

• Group membership should vary according to content and should not be fixed.

One approach to grouping students that many teachers and researchers feel is a good fit for inclusion is cooperative learning (Friend & Bursuck, 1998; King-Sears, 1998; Udvari-Solner & Thousand, 1996; Vaughn, Bos, & Schumm, 2000). As Udvari-Solner and Thousand (1996) have noted, there are three approaches to student interactions in classrooms: (1) individualistic (students working alone toward their own goals, with no concern for the progress of others); (2) competitive (students working to see who is the "best"); and (3) cooperative (students working together, each with a stake in the success of the others). While individual and competitive approaches "interfere with the building of community, which is a major objective of inclusive education" (Udvari-Solner & Thousand, 1996, p. 188), the cooperative method "transforms the classroom into a microcosm of the diverse society and work world that students will enter and into a place for acquiring the skills to appreciate and cope with people who initially might be perceived as 'different'" (p. 189).

Cooperative learning takes many forms, but they share common characteristics (Friend & Bursuck, 1998), including the following:

• Interdependence—group members depend on one another to reach a goal. They either reach the goal together, or no one reaches it.

• Face-to-face interactions—group members work together to achieve goals.

• Individual accountability—group members are individually accountable for their work in cooperative groups.

• Enhancing interpersonal skills—although much research supports the positive effect cooperative groups have on academic achievement (King-Sears, 1998), a principal reason to use cooperative groups is to foster peer relationships and enhance interpersonal relationships.

Many forms of cooperative learning have been used in inclusive classrooms, including Cooperative Integrated Reading and Composition (Jenkins, Jewell, Leicester, O'Connor, Jenkins, & Troutner, 1994);

Learning Together (Johnson & Johnson, 1991); Jigsaw (Aronson, Blaney, Stephan, Sikes, & Snapp, 1978); Team-Assisted Individualization (Slavin, 1994); Student Teams—Achievement Divisions (Slavin, 1994); and Classwide Peer Tutoring (Delquadri, Greenwood, Whorton, Carta, & Hall, 1986). The approach to cooperative learning that has perhaps been most widely and successfully used in inclusive classrooms is Classwide Peer Tutoring. This approach to cooperative learning is "a procedure by which all students tutor each other in a reciprocal arrangement, with each student serving in the roles of tutor and tutee" (King-Sears, 1998). Classwide Peer Tutoring may be used to enhance content learning, promote diversity and integration, and free teachers to prepare for other instructional activities (Smith, Polloway, Patton, & Dowdy, 1998).

Another approach to grouping students for instruction that has not been widely used in inclusive classrooms but that seems to be a good "fit" for inclusion is multi-age grouping (King-Sears, 1998; Udvari-Solner & Thousand, 1996). Multi-age grouping entails including students from more than one grade level in a classroom. If multi-age grouping is to be successfully implemented, traditional views of learning—for example, that students at a given age level have similar needs and abilities and benefit from similar instruction, or that learning by grade level is a predictable, sequential, and orderly process—must be discarded. In contrast to these beliefs, the views supporting a multi-age approach to grouping would include perspectives such as the following: (1) the learning process is continuous and dynamic; (2) children are expected and encouraged to learn at different rates and levels; and (3) learning experiences should be designed that are developmentally appropriate, to meet the needs of a diverse range of students. The components of a multi-age classroom that make it effective for students without disabilities are the same components that make this grouping arrangement effective for students with disabilities. These components include an emphasis on heterogeneity, flexible grouping, a child-centered curriculum, and the use of differentiated instructional methods (Udvari-Solner & Thousand, 1996).

In sum, a critical criterion of the successful inclusive classroom is ensuring that each student is part of the learning community of the classroom. Significant changes in general education classrooms are required to meet this goal. These changes typically entail addressing the curriculum used in the classroom, the instructional methods used to deliver the curriculum, and the manner in which students are grouped as they are being taught. Ultimately, successfully engaging students with disabilities as part of the learning community of the classroom ensures that they are not only "in" the general education classroom but also "of" the classroom (Ferguson, 1995).

Making Substantial Modifications

Pugach (1995) states that even after a new curricular framework and "the most encompassing philosophy of learning" (p. 220) are in place to accommodate diversity in a classroom, "It is unrealistic to think that . . . students will cease to need intensive instruction" (p. 220). Much research exists to support this perspective. Although students with disabilities generally seem to do better academically in inclusive classes, some students make very little progress in these settings (Klingner, Vaughn, Hughes, Schumm, & Elbaum, 1998; Waldron & McLeskey, 1998). In addition, a small group of students in public schools are labeled with severe emotional or behavior disorders; the needs of these students are extremely difficult, if not impossible, to meet in the general education classroom, and they require intensive instruction (Kauffman, Lloyd, Baker, & Riedel, 1995). We will look at three examples of approaches that have been used to address the academic and social/behavioral needs of these students.

First, for young students who do not make adequate progress learning to read in well-designed, inclusive classrooms, the most thoroughly researched alternatives for meeting the needs of these students are intensive, early intervention programs such as Reading Recovery (Clay, 1985; Pinnell, Short, Lyons, & Young, 1986; Wasik & Slavin, 1993) and Success for All (Slavin, Madden, Dolan, Wasik, Ross, & Smith, 1994; Slavin, 1997). Both programs use one-on-one tutoring for 20–30 minutes a day; the intervention supplements general education classroom instruction; and well-trained teachers provide the instruction (Spear-Swerling & Sternberg, 1996). Brief descriptions of both programs follow.

Reading Recovery. Among all early intervention programs in reading, Spear-Swerling and Sternberg (1996) describe Reading Recovery as "the most frequently cited, perhaps one of the most effective, and certainly one of the most controversial" (p. 282). Much of the controversy regarding the program seems to relate to the cost of the program and the limited number of students who can be served in a school year (Spear-Swerling & Sternberg, 1996). Reading Recovery is one of the most widely used programs in inclusive schools where we have worked, and it is often strongly supported by teachers and administrators, although the expense and cost-effectiveness of the program are frequent concerns.

Reading Recovery entails identifying students in 1st grade who score in the lowest 20th percentile in reading in their classroom, and pulling them out of the classroom for 30 minutes of one-on-one tutoring each day. Reading Recovery teachers receive intensive training for one year before beginning the program and are extremely well trained in the use of the explicit, well-designed methods. Reading Recovery is viewed as a short-term intervention, and it is assumed that most students will catch up with 1st grade classmates within 12 to 20 weeks.

Reading Recovery emphasizes instruction in meaningful contexts, although reading decoding skills are taught directly. The tutorial periods are spent primarily engaging in four activities: rereading familiar books, writing, reading new books, and keeping a running record of the child's reading in context for the teacher, who uses this information to make instructional decisions. As Vaughn, Bos, and Schumm (2000) have noted, Reading Recovery is not a packaged program, and it requires few materials other than a pencil, paper, and books selected by the teacher that are on the student's reading level. Books that are used are carefully chosen for their natural language and predictable text. Although some have challenged the effectiveness of Reading Recovery, most of the available research reveals that this program results in very positive outcomes for many young children (Spear-Swerling & Sternberg, 1996; Wasik & Slavin, 1993).

Success for All. This program, also very widely used, is often part of inclusive school programs as they are developed and implemented. Success for All is built upon two essential principles (Slavin,

1997): (1) learning problems should be prevented whenever possible by providing the best possible classroom instruction; and (2) when learning problems are manifested, interventions should be used that are "immediate, intensive, and minimally disruptive to students' progress in the regular program" (p. 377).

Like Reading Recovery, Success for All requires that students be pulled out of their general education classroom and provided one-on-one reading tutoring for 20 minutes a day. This tutorial instruction is designed to support the general education curriculum rather than to address different objectives. Tutorial work is not done during classroom instruction in reading and language arts. In contrast to Reading Recovery, Success for All is used for students in grades K–3. Tutoring sessions typically consist of reading "familiar stories, drill on letter sounds, reading of stories with controlled vocabulary, and writing activities" (Vaughn, Bos, & Schumm, 2000, p. 325).

A second aspect of Success for All is regrouping all students for reading and language arts instruction during 90-minute blocks of time. Students are regrouped across grade levels for instruction, so that 10 to 20 students who are on a similar reading level are grouped together. Classroom teachers and tutors are used as instructors for these groups, to allow for reduced class sizes.

The curriculum for Success for All, which is consistent for the tutorial and reading group instruction, consists of instruction in phonics, reading comprehension, and listening comprehension (Vaughn, Bos, & Schumm, 2000) and is designed to take full advantage of having 90 minutes of direct instruction (Slavin, 1997). In kindergarten, the program emphasizes the development of basic language skills and letter/sound recognition skills. In 1st grade, an approach based on sound blending and phonics is used, with an emphasis on oral reading to partners and the teacher. Finally, in grades 2 and 3, cooperative learning (a form of Cooperative Integrated Reading and Comprehension [CIRC]) is used, in which students engage in activities related to "instruction in story structure, prediction, summarization, vocabulary building, decoding practice, writing, and direct instruction in reading comprehension skills" (Slavin, 1997, p. 379).

As with Reading Recovery, Success for All is frequently used in inclusive schools where we have worked and is often strongly supported by teachers and administrators, although the expense and cost-effectiveness of the program are frequent concerns. Much of the research regarding Success for All suggests that the program results in very positive outcomes for many students who are at risk for reading problems (Spear-Swerling & Sternberg, 1996).

A third approach used to provide intensive support for students with disabilities in secondary schools is direct instruction in the use of strategies for learning (Schumaker, Deshler, & Ellis, 1986). For students at the secondary level, it is widely recognized that many students with disabilities have academic, social, and vocational needs that cannot be met in traditional academic classrooms. Many of these students take classes in vocational high schools, work in job settings in the community, or take classes that provide instruction in survival skills (Zigmond, 1990) or life skills (Polloway, Patton, Epstein, & Smith, 1993). Time is needed for transition planning as students learn functional skills they will need in job and community settings. In addition, several factors make it difficult to include students with disabilities in secondary content-area classes. These factors include the emphasis on complex curricular material, the large gap in the skill levels of students, the widespread use of teacher-centered classrooms that emphasize lecture, and student characteristics as they proceed through adolescence (Cole & McLeskey, 1997). These factors likely contribute to teacher perceptions that they have very little time to adapt to the needs of students with disabilities (as well as others who do not learn the curriculum at the expected pace) (Scanlon, Deshler, & Schumaker, 1996; Tralli, Colombo, Deshler, & Schumaker, 1996). One approach that has met with some success in addressing these issues is a Strategies Intervention Model (Schumaker, Deshler, & Ellis, 1986).

The Strategies Intervention Model. It is widely accepted that many students with disabilities lack the skills to cope with the academic and social demands of secondary classrooms (Cole & McLeskey, 1997; Schumaker, Deshler, & Ellis, 1986). Students with disabilities often lack skills such as listening and note taking, test taking, monitoring their understanding of material, and independent problem solving. Schumaker, Deshler, and Ellis have developed several strategies designed to teach students skills that allow them to cope with the demands of secondary content-area classrooms. These strategies have typically been taught in resource classes, after which students apply the information in general education content-area classes. Much evidence suggests that students have been successful in learning and applying these strategies (Rieth & Polsgrove, 1998; Schumaker, Deshler, & Ellis, 1986).

With the movement toward inclusive schools, several attempts have been made to have general education teachers integrate strategy instruction into content-area instruction (Ellis, 1993; Scanlon, Deshler, & Schumaker, 1996; Tralli, Colombo, Deshler, & Schumaker, 1996). One such strategy was developed by Scanlon, Deshler, and Schumaker (1996) for use with middle school students. This procedure is called the ORDER strategy:

O—Open your mind and take notes.

R—Recognize the structure or organization of the content.

D—Design an organizer for the expository information.

E—Explain the information that has been organized to the teacher, a peer, or other assistant.

R—Recycle the information to study for a test or create a written product.

Scanlon and colleagues attempted to have content area teachers instruct students in the use of this strategy in several social studies classrooms. This procedure was used with limited success, as teachers had difficulty finding the time to teach the learning strategies and students made limited use of the ORDER strategy.

One of the difficulties in using the Strategies Intervention Model in inclusive classrooms is that many secondary content-area teachers feel that they do not have the time to teach these strategies (Tralli, Colombo, Deshler, & Schumaker, 1996). Although attempts to integrate strategy instruction into content-area instruction have met with some success (Ellis, 1993; Scanlon, Deshler, & Schumaker, 1996; Tralli, Colombo, Deshler, & Schumaker, 1996), most professionals agree that the best approach for teaching strategies to students with disabilities is "to teach students with disabilities strategies in the resource room, and then teach all students a brief, adapted version of relevant strategies in general education classes" (Tralli, Colombo, Deshler, & Schumaker, 1996, p. 215). Thus, when students with disabilities are included in content-area classes in secondary schools, the need often remains for a resource setting where more intensive instruction can be provided so that students can learn strategies for coping with content-area classroom demands.

It is important to note that this text has provided brief descriptions of only three programs that can be used to provide intensive instruction or support for students with disabilities in elementary and secondary schools. Additional alternatives for providing intensive support are included in the resource information in the appendix.

In conclusion, perhaps the most difficult task related to the creation of an inclusive school is to provide supports so that all students are part of the academic community of the classroom. *Curricular and instructional adaptations are a must if this is to occur.* In addition, even with the best available adaptations, some students will continue to need intensive instruction that is not typically provided for all students in the general education classroom. However, we have found that if major adaptations are made in curriculum and instruction of the general education classroom, using approaches similar to those described, most academic needs can be met, ensuring that students are full and successful participants in the academic community of the general education classroom.

Addressing Students' Social Needs in Inclusive Classrooms

One of the primary goals of inclusion is to provide students with disabilities with the opportunities needed to learn to get along with others, make friends, and build social networks that will provide them with support throughout their school career and beyond (Falvey, 1995; Jorgensen, 1998a, b; Snell, 1990). Active participation in the social community of the classroom is necessary if these goals are to be achieved. This participation is significantly facilitated if the student with a disability fits into the ebb and flow of the classroom much as other students fit in. This occurs if the student's rhythm of the day is similar to that of other students, if supports that are provided the students are natural and unobtrusive, and, in short, if difference becomes an ordinary part of the classroom, so that the student with a disability does not unnecessarily stand out from his or her peers.

Participation in the Academic Community of the Classroom

While many factors influence the extent to which a student is an active and successful member of the *social* community of a classroom, we have found that it is very difficult to engage a student in the social community of the classroom if she/he is not a member of the *academic* community of the classroom. Providing students with the opportunity to work along with others on academic tasks in the classroom provides a sense of belonging, helps to make the student feel that he/she is part of the classroom, reduces the stigma associated with the student's disability, reduces the occurrence of behavior problems, and provides the student with many opportunities to learn to get along with others and make friends. Thus, if a student is not an "active and equal participant in activities performed by the peer group" (p. 340), it is difficult for the student to become part of the social community of the classroom (Cullinan, Sabornie, & Crossland, 1992). Consider the following example:

EXAMPLE

One of the authors was observing in a 4th grade classroom as the students prepared for a geography test. The content of the test related to states in the southern United States, and one of the objectives was for the students to learn the names and capitals of the states. To facilitate learning this material, the teacher had grouped students into cooperative groups. The groups were working to ensure that all knew each of the states and their capitals. Some groups were using textbooks to drill others, others had maps of the United States and were filling in the names of the states and capitals, and still others were engaged in word games to learn the assigned material. During these activities, I noticed that one student was sitting alone, cutting shapes from a piece of paper. Noticing that I was watching this student from afar, the teacher said that the student was "emotionally handicapped" and was thus working alone. I approached the student and talked about what he was doing. He was cutting out shapes that appeared to be countries of the world and was not engaged in studying the southeastern states or their capitals. This student was not engaged in the learning or social community of the classroom.

It is obvious, at least during this activity, that this student was not a part of the academic or the social community of the classroom. Furthermore, if these types of learning activities continue, he will have few opportunities to learn to get along with others, make friends, and become an accepted member of the social community of the classroom. Rather, the student will likely be ostracized by others for his lack of participation in regular class activities, or perhaps ridiculed and treated with open hostility by other students—at least in part because of his lack of involvement in classroom activities. This lack of involvement in the classroom learning community also frequently results in student behavior problems that further alienate the student from his or her peers. Consider the following example:

EXAMPLE

Several years ago, the authors interviewed a number of teachers, before they developed inclusive classrooms, about the challenges that concerned them as they began this process. A major concern was that many students with disabilities would create behavior problems that would disrupt the classroom and make it difficult to create a positive climate for learning. After the inclusive schools had been in place for one year, the authors did follow-up interviews with the teachers. One of the noteworthy aspects was that teachers seldom mentioned behavior problems. We reminded the teachers that they had anticipated behavior problems as the program was being planned and asked them why they didn't mention them now. Their response was that the behavior of the students with disabilities, as a whole, was at least as good as the behavior of the students who were not labeled with disabilities. They attributed this, in large part, to the positive learning environments in the classroom: the students felt that they were part of the classroom and were learning, making progress, and being successful academically. Thus, the positive learning environment was effective in preventing many behavior problems. One special education teacher commented that before, with mainstreaming programs, students with disabilities were often isolated in the classroom, did not work on the same types of academic activities as other students, and, when they did do the same work as others in the classroom, often were frustrated by their lack of progress and poor work. This isolation and frustration often led to behavior problems in the classroom. In contrast, students now felt not only that they could be a part of the general education classroom but that they could succeed academically in that setting. Their behavior improved.

Several authors have suggested that if students are to be successful as full participants in the classroom, certain basic human needs must be addressed. One of these needs is that students must feel competent (Deci & Ryan, 1985; Glasser, 1986; Kohn, 1996) or feel that they are part of the classroom learning community. Thus, if classrooms are adapted so that "difference becomes ordinary" and all students participate and feel successful as they participate, the need for competence will be met, the occurrence of behavior problems will be reduced, and the opportunities for students to participate in the social community of the classroom will be significantly increased.

Participation in the Social Community of the Classroom

Creating a learning community that students with disabilities can be part of is a major step toward creating successful inclusive classrooms—but it is not enough. As several authors have pointed out (Deci & Ryan, 1985; Glasser, 1986; Kohn, 1996), students also need to feel accepted in the classroom as full participants in activities, as connected to the teacher and other students. An extensive body of research indicates that although some students with disabilities are readily accepted by their peers without disabilities in general education classrooms, others are rejected by peers and have a difficult time adjusting (Cartledge & Johnson, 1996; Sale & Carey, 1995; Salend, 1998; Vaughn, Elbaum, & Schumm, 1996). Of course, this issue is not limited to students with disabilities. Moreover, in most classrooms there are several students who do not fit in well and who would benefit from changes to help them better fit into the social community of the classroom.

We have used an activity to help teachers and administrators examine how well students fit into the social community in their school and what can be done to help them better fit in (see Figure 7.1). The description and questions related to the Booby birds quickly lead to a lively discussion among teachers and administrators about who are and who are not the "chicks" in the "charmed circle" in their school. Many teachers and administrators are somewhat surprised at the conclusions they reach from this discussion.

—Figure 7.1—
CONSIDERING THE SOCIAL COMMUNITY OF THE SCHOOL

Blue-footed Booby birds, which are described in the book *Hen's Teeth and Horse's Toes* (Gould, 1983), get their name from their remarkable tameness, which, unfortunately, allows them to be easily caught and makes them vulnerable to predators. Boobies mark their nesting territory during the brooding season by depositing a circle of droppings on the ground. Once the bird's eggs hatch, her chicks develop inside this circle. Life remains happy and secure in this charmed if odoriferous family circle. However, if the baby chick wanders beyond the protection of the circle, the result is often fatal, because Booby parents nurture only the chicks within their circle. Thus, once a chick wanders outside the circle, these otherwise caring and dedicated parents no longer recognize it as their own and do not feed it. This story has an even stranger twist. When food supplies are scarce, an older and stronger chick may deliberately push the younger sibling out of the circle and into starvation. Incredibly, as this occurs the Booby parents look on with pride at their older child.

1. Who are the "chicks" (students) in your school who live in the "charmed circle"?
2. Who are the chicks in your school who are *not* in the charmed circle?
3. Do students in your school move into and out of the charmed circle? How does this occur?
4. Do some chicks face educational malnutrition or starvation in your school?
5. What recommendations would you make to help change your school so that more chicks remain in the charmed circle?
6. What does this story have to say about education in general?

Most often, these discussions lead to clear ideas about the students who are and are not well connected to the social community of the school. We typically conclude the discussion by brainstorming how *all* students can be made more a part of a school's social community. Four factors are essential: (1) provide a classroom climate that promotes positive behaviors; (2) teach students about disabilities; (3) provide opportunities for students to learn social skills; and (4) provide opportunities for students to develop friendships.

Providing a Classroom Climate That Promotes Positive Behaviors

Students with disabilities are more likely to become part of the social community of the classroom if they have opportunities to interact in a positive manner, learn appropriate social behaviors from positive classroom models, and make friends and learn to get along with others in the classroom. Furthermore, students must know what is expected of them in the classroom and that the classroom is a safe, predictable setting. Many authors have written about how to achieve a positive classroom climate and manage student behavior (Carpenter & McKee-Higgins, 1998; Charles, 1996; Emmer, Evertson, Clements, & Worsham, 1997; Evertson, Emmer, Clements, & Worsham, 1997; Friend & Bursuck, 1998; Salend, 1998; Smith & Rivera, 1998). Most of these approaches have certain features in common:

- Establishing a climate of trust and fairness in the classroom.
- Involving students in classroom management decisions.
- Establishing rules for classroom behavior that are learned by all students.
- Anticipating discipline problems and intervening before they occur.
- Managing the instructional environment, including transitions, to prevent student discipline problems.
- Designing specific intervention techniques for use when discipline problems occur.

In short, a predictable, safe school environment provides a setting in which students have more opportunities to make friends, learn positive social behaviors from others, and become part of the social community of the classroom. For more detailed information, see the resources described in the appendix.

Teaching Students About Disabilities

Research on peer attitudes toward students with disabilities reveals that many students who do not have disabilities have negative attitudes toward persons with disabilities (Salend, 1998). If negative attitudes are to be changed and social rejection is to be avoided, teachers must directly address student attitudes toward persons with disabilities. Many resources may be used to address this issue, including simulations of disabilities (Hallenbeck & McMaster, 1991; Salend, 1998); use of books, videos, and movies (McGookey, 1992); and use of instructional materials to teach students about disabilities (Barnes, Berrigan, & Biklen, 1978). Professional organizations can provide useful information and guest speakers to address these issues. For more information, see the appendix.

Social Skills Instruction

"Social skills can be thought of as the behaviors that help students interact successfully with peers, teachers and others and that help students win social acceptance" (Friend & Bursuck, 1998, p. 479). Research suggests that an estimated 10 percent of the school-age population has difficulties with social skills that may lead to peer rejection and that this figure is much higher among students with disabilities (Sugai & Lewis, 1998). Furthermore, research has shown that many students with disabilities have persistent problems with their social interactions, that these problems result from a lack of appropriate social skills, and that students with disabilities (as well as many other students) benefit from direct instruction in social skills (Kavale & Forness, 1996; Sugai & Lewis, 1998). Indeed, direct instruction in social skills may be necessary for some students with disabilities if they are to get along with peers and become part of the social community of the general education classroom. In addition, we have found that direct instruction in social skills benefits many other students in the general education classroom and results in an improved classroom environment.

Many programs for social skills instruction are available that can be conveniently built into the school day as part of ongoing instructional activities (please see the appendix). In addition to direct instruction of social skills, many professionals have found that students may learn social skills through their participation as peacemakers (Udvari-Solner & Thousand, 1996), using programs such as peer mediation (Salend, 1998; Schrumpf, 1994). When conflicts arise, peer mediators "attempt to facilitate conflict resolution through communication, problem solving, and critical thinking through role plays and practice" (Salend, 1998, p. 418).

Friendships

According to Cullinan, Sabornie, and Crossland (1992), one of the criteria to determine if a student is fully integrated socially into a classroom is whether he or she has at least one reciprocal friendship. Indeed, it is difficult to imagine a student as a full participant in the social community of the classroom who does not have a friend in the classroom. Falvey and Rosenberg (1995) have pointed out that it is difficult to provide a simple definition of friendship. They go on to note that while the specific definition of friendship depends on the age and other characteristics of the friends, friendships tend to be characterized by qualities such as interdependence, connectedness, equality, give-and-take, and support. "Friends are characterized by a wide range of social interactions. Friends engage not only in reciprocal interactions (i.e., give-and-take), but also in helping (i.e., voluntary assistance) and proximal interactions (i.e., interactions during which only sensory contact is made between two people)" (Falvey & Rosenberg, 1995, p. 268).

Students with disabilities are more likely to make friends with others if they are active participants in the learning and social communities of the classrooms. However, under the best of circumstances, direct involvement or support from the teacher may be needed to ensure that friendships develop. As Friend and Bursuck (1998) have noted, having students interact is a start, but it is often not enough. "The second component in building social relationships is to nurture mutual support and friendship between students with and without disabilities" (p. 455). Educators can encourage friendships, for example, through heterogeneous cooperative groupings, peer support committees, and get-acquainted activities (Salend, 1998). Stainback, Stainback, and Wilkinson (1992) have suggested that friendships may be facilitated if instruction about friendships is made an integral part of the curriculum. Units and programs designed to teach about friends have been developed and may be useful for classroom teachers as they address this topic. Finally, two widely used approaches for teaching students about friendships and support systems for students with disabilities are Circle of Friends (Snow & Forest, 1987) and Special Friends (Voeltz et al., 1983). For more information about these and other resources for building friendship, see the appendix.

Intensive Interventions for Students with Challenging Behaviors

We recognize that the vast majority of discipline problems can be addressed in the general education classroom, especially if it has been adapted to support a diverse range of student needs and if an effective approach to classroom discipline is in place. In short, if students think that they are part of the learning and social community of the school, many potential behavior problems will be prevented, and those that do occur will be addressed effectively. Even under the best of circumstances, however, we have found that a small number of students' needs cannot be met in the general education classroom. Consider the following vignette.

EXAMPLE

Tom, a 3rd grader with serious academic deficits, has exhibited severe behavior problems with every teacher he has had. In 1st grade, he frequently urinated in the classroom and other inappropriate places and picked fights with other children. Now, not only is he highly aggressive, but he also frequently steals from the teacher and his classmates and is labeled a thief by his peers. His mother does not see his stealing as a serious problem; his father is in jail. Neither Tom nor his mother is receiving any counseling or mental health services. The school's prereferral team has found no strategy to control his aggressive behavior. In the middle of his 3rd grade year, Tom was placed with an exceptionally strong male teacher, who finds it impossible to control Tom's behavior and to teach the rest of his class at the same time. This teacher wants Tom to be evaluated for special education (Kauffman, Lloyd, Baker, & Riedel, 1995, p. 543).

It is important to recognize that in any school setting, there are some students whose needs cannot be met in the general education classroom. Many of these students, like Tom, are highly aggressive and disruptive and make it difficult, if not impossible, for anyone to receive a good education as long as they are in a general education classroom. These students need intensive, highly specialized services to address severe, pervasive, and chronic needs. Of course, the purpose of these services should be, at least in part, to provide the student with the social skills and behavioral control to successfully function in and benefit from "real-world" settings such as the general education classroom. However, to achieve this goal, it is often necessary to provide intensive services that cannot be offered while the student is in a general education classroom.

Kauffman and colleagues (1995) have suggested several characteristics of successful programs for students with severe emotional or behavior disorders that vividly illustrate the need to provide these services in a setting outside the general education classroom. For example, they note that successful programs are intensive and multifaceted, including as they do services to address all aspects of the problem, including "academic and social skills, social and family service, counseling or psychological therapy, and pharmacological treatment as necessary" (p. 544). Furthermore, teachers must coach students in, and allow them frequent opportunities to practice, the actual skills they need to develop in a safe setting. Finally, Kauffman and his colleagues note that interventions should not be "one-shot" interventions; rather, it should be assumed that these students' problems are not transient or simple to overcome but may require prolonged, if not lifelong, support services. It is obvious from this description that highly trained specialists are needed to provide the services needed by some students who are labeled with serious emotional or behavior disorders and that it will be necessary and appropriate at times to provide these services outside the general education classroom.

In conclusion, an integral part of any successful inclusion program is the development of classrooms and schools in which all students, including those with disabilities, have many opportunities and supports that allow them to become active participants in the social community of the school. Providing appropriate supports so that students are part of the academic community of the classroom is a good beginning, but it is not enough. Classroom climates need to promote positive behaviors, teach students about disabilities, provide social skills instruction as needed, and ensure that students have many opportunities to build friendships. These factors will go a long way toward ensuring that most students are part of the social community of the classroom.

8 Developing Inclusive Secondary Schools: Examples from Practice

The preceding chapters provide examples from secondary schools, but most are from elementary schools. The obvious reason is that a great many more inclusive programs have been developed in elementary schools than in secondary schools (Cole & McLeskey, 1997). Although no single reason arises, several educators have suggested that many factors contribute to the difficulty in developing and implementing inclusive programs in secondary schools. These include issues such as curriculum demands, the need for students to apply basic skills to learn, school organization, school culture, and pressure from outside agencies. After looking at these issues, we examine approaches that secondary schools have used to successfully develop inclusive school programs, in spite of the issues.

Difficulties in Developing and Implementing Inclusive Secondary Programs

Curriculum Demands

At the secondary level, classes focus on specific content areas, and students are expected to master a broad range of curricular material in some depth. For example, there is increasing emphasis on science as students move through the secondary school years—courses in basic science, biology, chemistry, and physics. Not only are secondary schools responsible for curricular content such as science, mathematics, and English across a range of skill levels, but they must also provide instruction about careers/vocations, functional living skills, survival skills, transition from high school to a variety of settings, and so forth. Thus, expectations are placed on teachers and students to master a broad range of diverse curricular content during the secondary school years, with increasing demands as students move from one grade level to the next.

The Need for Students to Apply Basic Skills to Learn Curricular Material

As demands are placed on students to master increasingly broad and complex curricular material in secondary schools, an assumption is made that basic skills such as reading, writing, and arithmetic have been mastered and will be applied to learn or demonstrate mastery of this content. This is often not the case for students with disabilities (and many other students, for that matter), as they lack the basic academic skills as well as the learning skills and strategies necessary for success (Cole & McLeskey, 1998; Rieth & Polsgrove, 1994; Schumaker & Deshler, 1988; Zigmond, 1990). Further contributing to the difficulties faced by secondary teachers is the much greater range of skill levels in their classes than is the case in elementary schools, and secondary schools are often not well equipped for teaching these basic skills.

School Organization

Most secondary schools are organized into six or seven class periods, each about 55 minutes, with students moving from one teacher to another during each class period. Thus, one teacher may teach five different classes, for a total of 125–175 students during a typical school day. Such a schedule leaves little time for teachers to get to know students well and to make adaptations or provide support based on individual student needs. Some schools have begun to address this issue by developing alternatives such as teaming or blocking in middle schools to create smaller communities of learners (Williamson, 1996) and block scheduling in high schools

(Canady & Rettig, 1993). Both of these alternatives have been particularly useful as inclusive programs have been developed (Gritzmacher & Larkin, 1993; Weller & McLeskey, in press).

School Culture

"The prevailing culture in many secondary schools supports a content-centered more than a student-centered orientation toward education. As a result, steps to accommodate the needs of students with disabilities are not top priorities of teachers and administrators" (Tralli, Colombo, Deshler, & Schumaker, 1996, p. 204). It is likely that school organization and curricular demands contribute to this prevailing perspective. In addition, most secondary teachers are trained as content-area specialists and place great emphasis on teaching specified content to large groups of students. Thus, some of these teachers cannot or are not inclined to make adaptations for students with disabilities who do not master the curricular content. Finally, teachers who are content-area specialists may be frustrated by the limited, slow progress made by students with disabilities (Smith, Polloway, Patton, & Dowdy, 1998).

Pressure from Outside Agencies

Secondary school administrators and teachers are directly and indirectly pressured by a wide array of outside individuals and agencies, including state legislatures, colleges and universities, the general public, businesses, and so forth. Secondary teachers and administrators have far less control over the curriculum offered in their schools than do teachers in elementary schools, and they are held to much more specific (and perhaps higher) standards for accountability (e.g., student SAT scores, completion of Carnegie units for graduation, and gateway tests that must be passed before graduation).

Given these factors, it is understandable that inclusive schools have been slow to develop at the secondary level. And the lack of existing programs has led to some controversy regarding just what inclusive programs at this level should entail. Most seem to agree that secondary programs should differ from elementary programs and that students should not necessarily spend the entire school day in general education classrooms. For example, some students should spend time in community/work settings (York & Reynolds, 1996), while other students should be placed in settings outside the general education classroom where more intensive supports can be provided (Kauffman, Lloyd, Baker, & Riedel, 1995). In addition, given the high rate at which students with disabilities are unsuccessful (or fail) in general education classrooms and drop out of school (Blackorby & Wagner, 1996; Rieth & Polsgrove, 1994; Schumaker & Deshler, 1988), it seems apparent that general education classrooms must be transformed so that the organization, curriculum, and instruction provided are designed to meet the needs of a diverse group of students (Deshler & Schumaker, 1988).

The following sections describe approaches that secondary schools have used to develop successful inclusive programs. These examples are not provided as models of how inclusion ought to be implemented in secondary schools. Rather, they illustrate how schools have built on their unique strengths and dispositions to develop inclusive programs that accommodated many students with disabilities in general education classrooms.

Examples from Inclusive Secondary Schools

The following examples are composites from several secondary schools. Topics addressed include (1) curricular decisions—what should be taught to students with disabilities, and how should limited resources be used; (2) the development of partnerships as the foundation for secondary inclusive programs; (3) altering the school day to better meet student needs; and (4) developing instructional communities as the foundation for inclusive programs.

Curricular Decisions

One of the critical decisions that secondary school faculties must make as they begin to develop inclusive programs is what curricular content will be emphasized for students with disabilities. In short, with the limited resources available to provide instruction for students with disabilities, what should they be taught, how should the instruction be delivered, and how should special education teachers spend their time? The following example is from Roosevelt High School, located in a Midwestern city with a population of approximately 70,000 (Cole, 1995; Cole & McLeskey, 1997). The school has an enrollment of 1,350 students, 93 percent of whom are Caucasian, 4.5 percent Asian American, 2 percent African American, and a small number of international students. Roosevelt reflects a rich blend of small urban, suburban, and rural communities in the area, and a large state university is located nearby. The high school has a faculty of 90 general education teachers and 10 teachers of students with disabilities. This example explains the rationale behind the curricular decisions the faculty made as they developed an inclusive program. It is important to note that these decisions were very difficult, involved compromise, and continue to be reflected upon and adjusted to ensure a good fit with the student population.

The staff at Roosevelt High School decided not to offer separate special education classes in basic academic skill areas (reading and mathematics) for four basic reasons. First, teachers recognized that students at Roosevelt with mild to moderate disabilities already had spent at least eight years (and more in many cases) receiving instruction in basic skills. Further, this instruction most often had resulted in continuing poor performance as well as a high level of frustration when these students addressed these topics in separate special education classrooms. The staff was also aware that previous pull-out basic skills instruction at Roosevelt had not been effective. As Zigmond (1990) has so aptly stated, students with learning disabilities tend to enter high school three to five years behind actual grade placement, and "unfortunately . . . do not seem to recoup these basic skill deficiencies during their years of attending secondary school resource programs . . . and, in fact, the gap between achievement scores and grade expectancy level actually seems to widen as students with learning disabilities progress through high school" (p. 5). Thus, the experience of the teachers at Roosevelt and the experiences of others suggested that there had to be a better alternative for students with mild to moderate disabilities than to continue instruction in basic skills through the high school years.

Second, the faculty at Roosevelt realized that if students were in basic skills classes, they would miss important opportunities to be exposed to a rich curriculum, cooperative learning experiences, and classroom discussions. Third, the faculty felt that the special education teachers could better spend their time in other activities (which will be subsequently described) that would provide greater benefits for students with disabilities, rather than continuing to provide instruction in basic skill areas.

Finally, evidence seemed to indicate that literacy skills learned in isolation (i.e., in separate reading classes) tended not to transfer to other academic or vocational content areas (Mikulecky, Albers, & Peers, 1994; Mikulecky & Lloyd, 1993). This finding, as well as experiences of the faculty at Roosevelt that supported this contention, led the faculty to decide that literacy and numeracy skills could best be taught within the context of content-area classes (i.e., English, science, vocational classes, and so forth), rather than teaching reading and basic mathematics as separate subject areas. Thus, it is important to note, the faculty did not "give up" on teaching literacy and numeracy skills to students with disabilities. For example, students would learn new vocabulary in an auto mechanics or social studies class, read books in English classes, learn math skills in a practical mathematics class, and participate in a variety of other activities to increase literacy and numeracy skills.

· General and special education faculty who worked with students with disabilities at Roosevelt recognized the importance of tutorial services for students with disabilities. These services helped students organize their work, complete homework, study for tests, learn study skills related to content-area subjects, and so forth. It was also readily apparent that support services were also needed by many students who were not labeled with disabilities. To address this need, a schoolwide program to provide tutoring to all students who needed these services was developed, involving administrators, teachers, paraprofessionals, peer tutors, and volunteers.

Teachers also considered the range of skill areas that could be taught to students with disabilities to better prepare them for the world after school, including content such as learning strategies, survival skills, life skills, and transition planning. A decision was made that this content was best taught within the context of ongoing classes, which provided a natural setting for teaching and applying these skills. Indeed, some of the general education classes were transformed to offer some aspects of these curricular areas to a wide range of typical students as well as to students with disabilities. Thus, separate special education classes addressing these topics were discontinued.

Vocational opportunities for students with mild to moderate disabilities continued to be offered through an area vocational school that was located on the campus of Roosevelt High School. The teachers of students with disabilities worked collaboratively with vocational staff and school counselors to develop these programs. One major change that did occur in the vocational program resulted primarily from the success of the program for students with substantial needs. These students were gaining important employment opportunities through a community-based and community-supported employment/work study program. It was obvious to faculty that students with mild to moderate disabilities would benefit substantially from similar experiences. Thus, the community-based work study program was expanded to include students with mild to moderate disabilities, and they were provided on-the-job training and community access skills during the school day.

Finally, the foundation for the program in special education at Roosevelt High School was built on partnerships between general education teachers and teachers of students with disabilities, as they transformed the content of general education classroom to better meet the needs of all students, including those with disabilities. (These partnerships will be described in detail later in this chapter.) It is important to note that this approach to delivering instruction represented a significant departure from previous practice, as teachers changed their perspectives regarding what this type of program should entail as the partnerships evolved. Before the development of the inclusive school program, "compensatory and support" programs were viewed as the primary support services provided by the teacher of students with disabilities to allow students with mild disabilities to succeed in the general education classroom. Such programs did not question the curriculum, instruction, or classroom organization of the general education classroom. Thus, "the problem" was perceived to reside within the student, and the role of the teacher of students with disabilities was viewed as making sure the student could fit into the general education classroom. As partnerships evolved, teachers quickly concluded that this perspective had to change. They found that while students with mild to moderate disabilities indeed lacked some of the skills manifested by typical students, these deficits could best be addressed by changing the general education classroom and by assisting students with disabilities within these settings to gain the skills necessary to succeed. Thus, as part of these partnerships, teachers worked to transform the general education classroom to better meet the needs of *all* students. These partnerships often resulted in significant changes in the curriculum of the general education classroom, the methods of delivering instruction, and the classroom organization. Classes also often became more student-centered and less teacher-centered or content-centered. The following section provides more information about these teaching partnerships, as well as an illustration of how this change occurred in one math class at Roosevelt High School.

Altering the School Day

As the preceding information reveals, the faculty and administration at Roosevelt High School made clear decisions about how special education teachers would spend their time and the curricular emphasis for providing instruction for students with disabilities. After these decisions were made and the program was under way, the faculty began to question the traditional schedule of six 50-minute periods (Weller & McLeskey, in press). The faculty cited three primary reasons to move to an alternative schedule: (1) to change the school day to allow for more instruction time; (2) to adopt more learner-centered, facilitative, and collaborative teaching methods; and (3) to better meet the needs of all students.

With these needs in mind, the faculty decided to adopt a Block 8 schedule. This change involved reducing the number of class periods per day from six 50-minute periods to four 85-minute periods. Furthermore, classes were offered on alternating days, with students taking up to four classes on Monday, Wednesday, and every other Friday, and four additional classes on Tuesday, Thursday, and every other Friday. With this schedule, students can take up to eight courses per semester, compared with a maximum of six courses under the traditional schedule.

Teachers at Roosevelt spent one year preparing for the change to the Block 8 schedule by examining their curriculum and instructional methods, ensuring that they were adapted to the longer time periods and were more student-centered. After the first year of implementation, the teachers at Roosevelt felt that the Block 8 schedule was a success in many ways, and that block scheduling complemented and supported inclusion better than a traditional schedule (Weller & McLeskey, in press). Benefits of the Block 8 schedule included the following:

• Teachers were forced to examine their teaching strategies, as many recognized that lecturing to students for 85 minutes was not going to work; in doing so, they began to develop lessons that focused more on cooperative and participatory learning activities.

• More opportunities were offered for teachers and students to get to know one another, which allowed teachers to get to know their students' individual learning styles and personal interests.

• The opportunity was offered to take eight classes per semester rather than six. This was beneficial for all students but especially for those with disabilities, who could take more classes in areas where they had weak content skills.

Teachers at Roosevelt felt that the Block 8 schedule was especially beneficial for students with disabilities and other "nontraditional learners" whose needs were not being met in a traditional high school classroom. In addition, many teachers felt that the way students with disabilities were already being included in general education classrooms within a traditional six-period day "tailored itself really nicely to going to block." Specifically, teachers thought that having established team-teaching partnerships and being "comfortable sharing teaching responsibilities" before implementing a block schedule was a benefit and "made the transition to block really, really good."

Developing Teaching Partnerships

Given the day-to-day organization of many secondary schools (broken into discrete periods of time during which 25–35 students are taught a specific content area by one teacher), teachers have a great deal of autonomy about what they teach and how they deliver this information to students. Furthermore, general education teachers are most often categorized by their specializations (e.g., math, English, social studies, science) and frequently have in-depth knowledge in one of these specializations but not others. In contrast, special education teachers often have skills related to teaching students basic skills, adapting instruction for individual student needs, providing support for students (e.g., tutoring), and providing instruction in areas such as strategies for learning, studying and test-taking, life skills, and transition to adulthood. It is noteworthy that there is little overlap in the areas of expertise of general and special education teachers in secondary schools. For example, general education teachers often lack specific skills in adapting for specific student needs, while special education teachers often lack in-depth knowledge of content areas.

The autonomy of secondary-level teachers, as well as the complementary areas of expertise that general and special education teachers often have, makes collaborative teaching partnerships the foundation for developing inclusive programs (Cole & McLeskey, 1997). These partnerships provide teachers with the opportunity to work together to transform the organization, curriculum, and instruction of the general education classroom to better meet the needs of all students. Although many schoolwide issues that were discussed in previous chapters need to be addressed, inclusion often will not occur in secondary schools unless teachers have the opportunity to work closely together to transform classrooms to better meet the needs of all students. The appendix lists resources that teachers can use to develop successful teaching partnerships.

Developing Instructional Communities

Although the preceding information about curricular decisions, teaching partnerships, and scheduling has implications for both middle and high schools, a unique aspect of middle schools that merits further discussion is the use of instructional teams to deliver instruction. The following description of McDuffie Middle School illustrates how teachers in this school developed teams or instructional communities as the foundation for inclusive programs.

McDuffie Middle School is located in a small Midwestern city with a population of approximately 80,000. The community includes a number of large national corporations, and much attention is focused on providing resources to public schools. McDuffie enrolls approximately 860 students in grades 7 and 8.

Before developing an initiative designed to improve instruction for all students, McDuffie Middle School offered a very traditional educational program, organized much like that of a departmentalized high school. The school day was broken into six 55-minute instructional periods. Students were tracked into these classes in each of the core content areas (i.e., English, mathematics, science, and social studies) based on their measured achievement level. Students with disabilities were mainstreamed into general education classrooms if they could do the same work and pass the same tests as all the other students. Thus, few classroom adaptations were made for students with disabilities (or for other students) who could not meet expectations. As a result, most students with disabilities received their education in core content areas in a separate special education classroom.

The superintendent in McDuffie's school district was very "reform minded." When a vacancy in the principalship occurred at McDuffie, he hired an experienced principal who had led a reform movement in a middle school in a school district in a nearby city. This principal found that many teachers at McDuffie, including five of the six special education teachers, believed that changes were long overdue. They recognized that the tracking system was not working well for many students or their teachers, especially those who were teaching in the low tracks. Furthermore, the special education teachers felt that their program simply reflected the lowest track in a highly stratified school. McDuffie was also pressured to develop an inclusive program, because students who had participated in inclusive programs in local elementary schools were about to graduate to the middle school.

The teachers at McDuffie initially formed a team to study what was working well at their school, what was not working, and what the faculty and administration were willing to change. They also visited other schools that had previously reformed their programs and perused the professional literature looking for promising practices to adapt for use at McDuffie. Their readings led them to the report of the Carnegie Council on Adolescent Development (1989). Several of the report's recommendations came to serve as the foundation of the school improvement effort at McDuffie:

• Create small communities for learning where stable, close, mutually respectful relationships with adults and peers are considered fundamental for intellectual development and personal growth.

• Teach a core academic program that results in students who are literate, think critically, behave ethically, and assume the responsibilities of citizenship in a pluralistic society.

• Ensure success for all students through elimination of tracking by achievement level, promotion of cooperative learning, flexibility in arranging instructional time, and adequate resources for teachers.

• Empower teachers and administrators to make decisions about the experiences of middle grade students through creative control by teachers over the instructional program.

Based on these principles and what they had learned from their visits to other schools, the planning team developed a plan for changing the educational program at McDuffie. They then discussed these recommendations with the entire school community and adapted the plan based on feedback. The foundation for the changes endorsed by the school community became the formation of communities of learners.

First, to develop communities of learners, the faculty and administration at McDuffie agreed that instruction should be organized around interdisciplinary teams of teachers. Each team included teachers with expertise in English, mathematics, science, social studies, and special education. Students who were not labeled with disabilities in a given grade level were randomly assigned to each team. After these assignments were made, the special education teachers and a group of general education teachers representing each team met to discuss the assignment of students with disabilities. They ultimately decided that students with disabilities would be assigned to teams at each grade level based on their reading level. Students with the highest reading levels would be assigned to one team at a given grade level, those with the lowest reading levels to a second team, and those in the middle to a third team. The teachers agreed that the students with the highest reading levels needed the lowest level of support, so a special education teacher was assigned to this team half-time. The team with the students with the lowest reading levels needed the most support, so this team was assigned two paraprofessionals and one full-time and one half-time special education teacher. Finally, the middle level readers were assigned one special education teacher and one paraprofessional. In addition to these services, one special education resource room was kept open during the entire school day, with either a special education teacher or a paraprofessional in the room to provide support to students for whom sufficient supports could not be provided in the general education classroom.

Second, the schedule for the school day at McDuffie was modified to ensure that flexible blocks of time were available for creative instructional alternatives developed by the teams. The school day was broken into 10 periods, with teaching teams responsible for determining how this time (with the exception of special areas and lunch) would be used. Thus, teachers could vary the time they spent on different subject areas, team teach, develop peer tutoring programs, integrate subject matter across content areas, and implement a range of other innovative activities to better meet the needs of students on their team.

Third, teaching teams had a common planning time while students were in special area classes. During this time, the team planned cooperative activities, coordinated instruction and assignments, monitored student progress, and planned needed adaptations. Finally, each student was assigned an adult advisor. This provided the opportunity for teachers and students to develop sustained personal relationships, "which are essential to teaching well, and to provide guidance during the at-times turbulent period of early adolescence" (Carnegie Council, 1989, p. 37).

By developing communities of learners, the faculty and administration at McDuffie Middle School have been able to better meet the needs of all students in a supportive setting. Teachers have learned new skills from one another and have also participated in a number of professional development opportunities to learn new skills that they deem necessary to improve their contributions to their community of learners.

In conclusion, there is no doubt that inclusion programs in secondary schools must be quite different from those that are implemented in elementary schools. The complexity of secondary programs and the academic demands placed on students and their teachers demand that substantial changes be made in the way the instructional day is organized and how instruction is delivered. The examples we have provided are only a small sample of the alternatives that can be used to achieve the changes necessary to support a diverse range of students in secondary general education classrooms. More resource information for teachers and administrators in secondary schools to use as they develop inclusive programs is provided in the appendix.

9 A Systematic Approach for Developing, Implementing, and Monitoring Inclusive Schools

Based on our experiences, both successful and unsuccessful, working with schools as they have developed and implemented inclusive school programs, we recommend a systematic process. Such an approach greatly increases the probability that a successful inclusive school will be developed. Figure 9.1 presents the 10 steps that we will discuss. Although the particulars of each step will vary, most successful inclusive schools we have worked with have addressed each of these steps in one way or another. It is important to keep in mind that we are not recommending these steps as a prescription but, rather, as a framework to guide planning and decision making as inclusive schools are developed, implemented, and maintained. We encourage local schools to modify the steps and their sequence and to add additional steps as needed. In short, a systematic approach is needed, but it should be tailored to the individual needs of the local school.

Step 1. Begin with a Discussion of Schooling for All Students

As teachers, administrators, and other stakeholders begin to develop an inclusive school program, it is perhaps most important that they clearly understand what such a program entails. For example, major changes are required in the *entire* school to develop an inclusive school, including changes in the beliefs of stakeholders concerning schooling and students with disabilities, as well as changes in cur-

---

—Figure 9.1—

TEN STEPS IN DEVELOPING AN INCLUSIVE SCHOOL

1. Begin with a discussion of schooling for all students.
2. Form a team.
3. Examine your school.
4. Examine other schools.
5. Develop a plan for the inclusive school.
6. Review and discuss the plan with the entire school community.
7. Incorporate feedback from the school community regarding the plan for inclusion.
8. Get ready.
9. Implement the plan.
10. Monitor, evaluate, and change the inclusive program, as needed.

---

riculum, school organization, and the daily instructional practices of teachers. Understanding the pervasiveness of the changes required is necessary if stakeholders are to make a well-informed decision about their readiness for change. That is, are they willing to expend the energy and take the time required to significantly change their school? Will the outcomes be worth the effort?

If the stakeholders in the local school decide that they are ready for change, they should develop an initial vision statement to serve as a guide. Frequently, too much time is spent on strategic planning and "visioning." At this stage, stakeholders shouldn't get bogged down in philosophical discussions about issues that, in the final analysis, will work themselves out and have little bearing on the inclusive school (for example, should a school be "fully inclusive," whatever that means?). In-depth discussions of such issues should be avoided.

We suggest that stakeholders begin with a general statement of philosophy that includes *all* students to guide their deliberations, such as the following: "The goal of the inclusive school is to prepare and support teachers to better meet the needs of all students who enter their classrooms." Note that this statement addresses the needs of *all* students in a school, not just those with disabilities. Any school change that entails the scope and magnitude required with inclusion will influence the education of all students. Furthermore, such change should strive to improve the education of *all* students, not just one small group of students.

Finally, ongoing discussions among *all stakeholders* should continue about beliefs, attitudes, and understandings regarding teaching, learning, and schooling. Topics should include the purposes of schooling, instructional practices that support a diverse range of students in a general education classroom, and so forth. These discussions should help teachers, administrators, and other stakeholders explore different mind-sets about schooling and students with disabilities and ultimately move the school toward a shared vision of effective education for all students (Fullan, 1993; Goodman, 1995; Jenlink, Reigeluth, Carr, & Nelson, 1998).

Step 2. Form a Team

We recommend that as many teachers, administrators, and other stakeholders as possible be involved in developing, implementing, and monitoring the changes in the school. Such involvement ensures good communication, increases the likelihood that a broad range of the teaching staff will accept the changes, and ensures widespread ownership for the changes that are implemented. Ideally, every teacher and administrator should be involved in every aspect of developing, implementing, and maintaining an inclusive school. However, because of the many time demands placed on teachers and administrators, the process works best if a core inclusion planning team guides the necessary changes (Jenlink, Reigeluth, Carr, & Nelson, 1998).

The team selected should be representative of the school. For example, teachers with differing beliefs about inclusion, as well as different beliefs about curriculum and instruction (e.g., traditional vs. constructivist), should be included. Teachers across grade levels and assignments (e.g., general education, special areas, subject-area specialists, special education) should be represented. *Most important, the teams should be made up of teachers and others who are well respected in the school—individuals others would listen to and trust.* We have found that the size of these core teams varies, depending on the size of the school, among other factors. Typically, at least 5 team members are needed, and we have worked with effective teams with as many as 12 members.

Initially, team members should become very knowledgeable about the change process and develop skills in group process (Jenlink, Reigeluth, Carr, & Nelson, 1998). Remember that once this team begins guiding the change process, the team members can very easily come to be viewed as "outsiders" by other members of the school community. To guard against this, the core team must involve as many stakeholders as possible in every aspect of the change process. Additional teams of stakeholders may need to be formed to work on certain aspects of the change process or to collect information that will be shared with the school community.

The ultimate goal of the team is to guide the school community in developing and implementing a successful inclusive program. To achieve this goal, the team will do much of the groundwork to complete the eight steps that follow and will involve as many stakeholders from the school community as possible in each of these activities.

Step 3. Examine Your School

We have never worked with a school where the administration and faculty felt that they had sufficient resources to achieve all their goals. Invariably, inclusion is initially looked upon as "one more thing to do" and a potential drain on already limited resources. The school should be examined carefully by the core planning team to

- Ensure that the inclusive program is developed with sensitivity to existing workloads.
- Provide a foundation for determining how resources can be used more efficiently and effectively for all students.
- Provide stakeholders with the necessary information to develop a plan for inclusion that is tailored to the needs and preferences of the school community.

To address these issues, the core planning team should guide a two-step process, ensuring that as many members of the school community as possible are involved in these activities. First, it is necessary to collect information that provides a comprehensive description of the school (this step will be called Activity I). This information is then used to develop interviews (Activity II) with stakeholders (teachers, administration, parents, central office administrators, school board members, and others as appropriate) regarding their perspectives on inclusive schools and related issues.

The initial step in this process, Activity I, is outlined in Figure 9.2. In describing a school, many types of information should be collected to provide a full understanding of the current status of services and supports provided for students. The particular types of information will vary, depending on the setting but will normally include the following:

- General information about your school.
- Information regarding the inclusiveness of support services currently provided to students with disabilities.
- Information about school policies and practices that may influence an inclusive school.

The information in Activity I should be compiled by the core planning team and other stakeholders and used as the foundation for planning Activity II, interviews with stakeholders. Figure 9.3 presents an outline of this activity, which generates an understanding of stakeholders' perspectives about changes that can be made to develop an inclusive school. That is, what changes would teachers and administrators support as an inclusive school is developed and implemented?

Step 4. Examine Other Schools

The single best source of information about inclusive schools is most often other schools with similar populations who have successfully implemented inclusive programs. The core planning team and as many stakeholders from the school community as possible should visit a variety of inclusive schools. Visits to classrooms and interviews or group discussions with teachers can yield important information about the nuts and bolts of inclusive schools. Furthermore, as Roach (1995) has noted, "Many teachers have no mental picture of what it would be like to work in an inclusive setting" (p. 298).

—Figure 9.2—
ACTIVITY I: DESCRIBE YOUR SCHOOL

The purpose of this activity is to give the inclusion planning team the opportunity to explore factors within the school setting that may impede or enhance the successful inclusion of all students into the physical, academic, and social life of the school. Because this challenging task requires continual review and adaptation of practices, every school will have strengths as well as areas needing improvement. Therefore, papers completed by school-based teams *should not be considered a critique of school practices,* but rather *a needs assessment to determine possible directions for improving* the "hidden curriculum" in a school that impedes or enhances its success in including and meeting the needs of *all* students.

With the preceding ideas in mind, participants should work in school-based teams to respond to questions/issues such as the following:

General Information About Your School

1. *Description of Your School*

   - How many students are in your school?
   - What proportion are on free lunch?
   - What is the racial makeup of your school?
   - How many teachers are in your school?
   - What are class sizes?
   - Other information?

2. *Students with Disabilities in Your School*

   - How many students with disabilities are in your school?
   - Break out your students by grade level and disability label.
   - Are all of these students in their neighborhood or home school? Explain.
   - How many students with disabilities have your school as their home school?

3. *Supports for Students with Disabilities*

   - Describe the intensity of services currently provided to students with disabilities—that is, how many students receive consultation or indirect support only, part-time inclusive assistance, pull-out support, and so forth at each grade level?
   - Define the terms you use to describe intensity of services.

4. *Additional Support Services in Your School*

   - How many teachers, instructional assistants, volunteers, and so forth provide services for students with special needs in your school? Include any student who has needs that are not met in the general education classroom (e.g., gifted and talented, Title I, volunteer programs).
   - Describe teachers or other persons who provide support, type of support provided, and number of students served.

Students with Special Needs and Their Teachers

1. *Language Used (Is Inclusive Language Used?)*

   - Describe generally accepted terminology for students with disabilities and other students with special needs (e.g., Title I); names of special classes; sensitivity to the use of terms such as special education (e.g., "special education" over loudspeaker, listed on door, in school newsletter).

—continued—

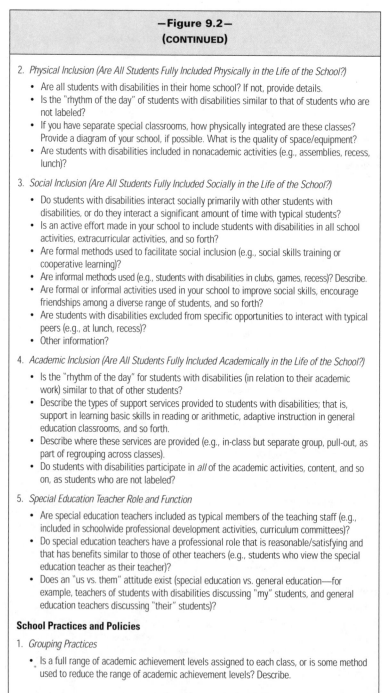

—Figure 9.2—
(CONTINUED)

2. *Physical Inclusion (Are All Students Fully Included Physically in the Life of the School?)*
   - Are all students with disabilities in their home school? If not, provide details.
   - Is the "rhythm of the day" of students with disabilities similar to that of students who are not labeled?
   - If you have separate special classrooms, how physically integrated are these classes? Provide a diagram of your school, if possible. What is the quality of space/equipment?
   - Are students with disabilities included in nonacademic activities (e.g., assemblies, recess, lunch)?

3. *Social Inclusion (Are All Students Fully Included Socially in the Life of the School?)*
   - Do students with disabilities interact socially primarily with other students with disabilities, or do they interact a significant amount of time with typical students?
   - Is an active effort made in your school to include students with disabilities in all school activities, extracurricular activities, and so forth?
   - Are formal methods used to facilitate social inclusion (e.g., social skills training or cooperative learning)?
   - Are informal methods used (e.g., students with disabilities in clubs, games, recess)? Describe.
   - Are formal or informal activities used in your school to improve social skills, encourage friendships among a diverse range of students, and so forth?
   - Are students with disabilities excluded from specific opportunities to interact with typical peers (e.g., at lunch, recess)?
   - Other information?

4. *Academic Inclusion (Are All Students Fully Included Academically in the Life of the School?)*
   - Is the "rhythm of the day" for students with disabilities (in relation to their academic work) similar to that of other students?
   - Describe the types of support services provided to students with disabilities; that is, support in learning basic skills in reading or arithmetic, adaptive instruction in general education classrooms, and so forth.
   - Describe where these services are provided (e.g., in-class but separate group, pull-out, as part of regrouping across classes).
   - Do students with disabilities participate in *all* of the academic activities, content, and so on, as students who are not labeled?

5. *Special Education Teacher Role and Function*
   - Are special education teachers included as typical members of the teaching staff (e.g., included in schoolwide professional development activities, curriculum committees)?
   - Do special education teachers have a professional role that is reasonable/satisfying and that has benefits similar to those of other teachers (e.g., students who view the special education teacher as their teacher)?
   - Does an "us vs. them" attitude exist (special education vs. general education—for example, teachers of students with disabilities discussing "my" students, and general education teachers discussing "their" students)?

School Practices and Policies

1. *Grouping Practices*
   - Is a full range of academic achievement levels assigned to each class, or is some method used to reduce the range of academic achievement levels? Describe.

—continued—

126

—Figure 9.2—
(CONTINUED)

- Are grouping arrangements for academic subjects heterogeneous or homogeneous? Describe.
- Does multi-age grouping occur? Describe.
- What options are available to assist students to better fit into groups (e.g., cooperative learning, curricular adaptation)?
- Are methods such as grade retention used to reduce the diversity of students in groups? Describe.
- How might these practices support or impede inclusion?

2. *Grading Policies*

- What are the grading policies in your school/corporation?
- How are effort, progress, mastery of content, and peer comparisons used in report card grading? What is emphasized most?
- Are grades adapted for students with disabilities? For other students with special needs? For students who do not have special needs? Describe.
- Do teachers feel free to make adaptations in grades? Are there (should there be) limits on the adaptations in grades that can be made (e.g., made only for students labeled with disabilities, or for all students)? Explain your response.
- Does a corporation-wide grading policy and/or report card exist?
- How might these practices support or impede inclusion?

3. *Testing Policies*

- How are students with disabilities and other special needs included in schoolwide testing activities?
- Are some students with disabilities excluded from school, system, or statewide testing programs? Describe.
- How might these practices support or impede inclusion?

4. *Curricular/Instructional Adaptations*

- Do teachers in your school commonly adapt curriculum and instruction in all classes?
- What types of adaptations are most common?
- Do teachers feel free to make curricular and instructional adaptations? Explain (e.g., if teachers do not feel free to make adaptations, why is this the case?).
- Are there limits on the adaptations that can be made (e.g., is everyone required to use a basal reading series)? Are adaptations made for *all* students, including those who are not labeled with a disability?
- How might these practices support or impede inclusion?

5. *Discipline Policies and Practices*

- Are there schoolwide rules for student behavior? Describe.
- Do teachers tend to have individual classroom rules? Describe.
- Do discipline policies differ for students with disabilities? Describe.
- How might these policies and practices support or impede inclusion?

6. *School Policies and Practices and Inclusion*

- What are the most important policies and practices in your school that might support inclusion?
- What are the most important policies and practices in your school that might impede inclusion?

Figure 9.3
ACTIVITY II: INTERVIEW STAKEHOLDERS

This activity entails interviewing persons in your school or school corporation who will be influenced by the changes you may make in your school and/or who will be influential in determining whether your planned changes are successfully implemented. Stakeholders include teachers, students, parents, school board members, and central office administration. Each team member should interview at least two stakeholders. In addition, the building principal should be interviewed. When the interviews are being written up, *names of those being interviewed should not be used.*

Activity I should provide a wealth of topics that can be the focus of these interviews. To get you started, the following are examples of topics that may be addressed in the interviews.

1. Attitudes, beliefs, and understandings of the school faculty and administration regarding inclusion.

   • Is inclusion a good idea?
   • Do students with disabilities benefit from inclusion?
   • Do typical students benefit from inclusion?
   • Should some students not be included?
   • Are you willing to accommodate for these students by adapting curriculum and instruction? Expectations? Grades? Classroom groupings? Discipline practices? Testing?
   • Do you have the time, resources, and expertise to successfully include students with disabilities?
   • Have your past experiences with inclusion or mainstreaming been mainly positive or negative?

2. Attitudes, beliefs, and understandings of other stakeholders (e.g., parents, central administration, school board members) about inclusion.

   • Is inclusion a good idea (do you support the concept of inclusion)?
   • Do students with disabilities benefit from inclusion?
   • Do typical students benefit from (or are they harmed by) inclusion?

3. What school policies and practices are in place to support inclusion? Address policies and practices related to topics such as:

   • Student grouping
   • Grading
   • Testing
   • Adaptation of curriculum and instruction
   • Discipline

4. What school policies and practices are in place that may impede the development of an inclusive program?

5. What changes will be needed in your school to better accommodate the needs of *all* students? Should your school be involved in these changes?

6. What are the strengths of your school that are in place to support inclusive programs?

7. What are the particular challenges that your school would face in developing or improving your inclusive program?

The following guidelines will help you during the interviews and write-ups:

   • During the interview, take notes that capture the critical elements of each response.
   • After each question, restate for the persons being interviewed what you perceive to be the critical elements of their responses.
   • Make changes and additions based on the responses in the previous item.
   • Immediately following the interview, make notes concerning your general impressions and reactions to the interview.
   • As soon as possible after the interview, prepare a written summary of the responses.

Site visits thus "are keys to providing a frame of reference for teachers" (p. 298).

These visits should be carefully planned to ensure that (1) a setting does indeed have a successful inclusive program; (2) the setting is appropriate with regard to size, student population, organization (teamed vs. departmentalized, or graded vs. multi-age), instructional philosophy (traditional vs. constructivist), and other factors; (3) teachers and administrators are able to observe in settings that will be particularly useful for them (a 1st grade teacher in a 1st grade classroom and not in a 6th grade classroom); and (4) faculty and administration who will have the most useful information can be interviewed.

One successful strategy that we have used is to schedule a half-day visit to a school. The day begins before children come into classrooms with a meeting with faculty and administration, who provide a brief description of the inclusive program. This is followed by scheduled visits to classrooms that are matched to the individual needs and interests of the visitors. Finally, the visit concludes with a debriefing session, in which teachers respond to questions that have arisen. Immediately following the school visit, core planning team members and other stakeholders meet to discuss the visit and reflect on what they have learned and how to use this information as they develop their own inclusive school.

Step 5. Develop a Plan for the Inclusive School

A detailed plan for the inclusive school should be developed, based on the resources, needs, and preferences that exist within the school community. The information collected in Steps 3 and 4 should serve as the foundation for this plan. While the core planning team should take the primary responsibility for guiding the development of this plan, it may be necessary to develop teams of stakeholders from the school community to develop different aspects of the plan. For example, in a middle school, teams of teachers who work together to teach groups of students will need to develop a plan that includes the particulars regarding how inclusion will work. We have also worked with teams in elementary schools where primary-level teachers (grades K–3) work together to develop a plan for their grade levels, while intermediate teachers (grades 4–6) work together with a similar purpose. In a high school, planning teams may be developed for each department or subject area (e.g., English or social studies). This type of organization for planning the inclusive school suggests that changes must be tailored to the individual needs of students and teachers at a given grade level or in a given subject area and that there is no one-size-fits-all approach that works for all stakeholders.

The plan for inclusion should provide a general framework that addresses issues such as where students will be placed in the school; how curriculum, instruction, and school organization will change to better meet student needs; and what type of supports will be provided in each classroom. The plan should also address other school-wide issues, including the following questions:

- How will curricular expectations be adapted for students with disabilities?
- How will individualized education programs (IEPs) be adapted?
- How will grading be adapted?
- How will students with disabilities be included in schoolwide testing?
- How will the plan be presented to the school staff?
- How will the plan be presented to parents?

Another major issue the plan should address is the professional development needs of the entire staff as they prepare for inclusion. The faculty should have the primary responsibility for determining professional development needs, but topics that are often addressed include the following:

- Why implement an inclusive school? How will it work? How well will it work?
- Collaboration, teaming, and coteaching.
- Instructional strategies and curricular adaptations.
- Alternative grouping strategies (e.g., cooperative learning, multi-age grouping).
- Understanding the change process.
- Schoolwide discipline, conflict resolution, and social skills training.

In addition to these professional development topics, faculty should be given the opportunity to visit sites where inclusive schools have been successfully developed, to participate in situation-specific problem-solving sessions (Roach, 1995), and to participate in other professional development activities, as needed.

Another component of the plan should be a framework for ongoing monitoring and evaluation once the changes are implemented. Such a plan should address, at a minimum, the academic and social progress made by students with disabilities; the academic and social progress made by students who are not labeled with disabilities; and teacher, parent, and administration satisfaction with the inclusive school.

Figure 9.4 provides an outline that core planning teams have followed as they developed a plan. It should be noted that this plan builds on the information that was collected in Activities I and II (Figures 9.2 and 9.3).

Step 6. Discuss the Plan with the Entire School Community

Once a draft plan for inclusion has been completed, the core planning team should review and discuss the plan with the entire school community. This step is needed to ensure that all stakeholders understand what is included in the plan, how the implementation of the plan will affect them, and whether the plan needs to be adapted to better meet student needs. It is important to note that core planning team members and other stakeholders who were most involved in developing the plan will feel the most ownership for the plan at this point. Indeed, participants in developing the plan will have many experiences and much knowledge about inclusion that other stakeholders do not have. This may lead some stakeholders to view those who developed the plan as "outsiders," and some resistance to the plan may occur.

The primary goal of the core planning team at this stage is to gain the trust of the majority of the faculty that the plan provides a reasonable framework to begin planning the nuts and bolts regarding how inclusion will work in particular classrooms. A

Figure 9.4
ACTIVITY III: DEVELOP A PLAN

This activity should be an outgrowth of Activities I and II; it will lead to a strategy and implementation plan for school change and improvement.

1. Describe your school, providing a context for the proposed school change and/or improvement.

2. Present a vision statement for your school that provides a context for the changes you are proposing.

3. Provide a detailed plan for school change and/or improvement for the coming school year or beyond, based on the resources, needs, and preferences within your school. The plan should address changes that will occur to better meet student needs, including issues such as:

   • Student placement
   • Teacher roles and responsibilities
   • School organization
   • Curriculum, instruction, grading, testing, IEPs
   • Student discipline
   • Teacher beliefs and understandings about teaching and learning

4. Analyze your school's systems:

   • Who are the people who will be most likely to support the proposal? Resist the proposal?
   • What logistical difficulties might the proposal impose on the staff?
   • Are there some "behavioral regularities" that will be challenged by the proposed changes (e.g., grading or discipline policies, grouping patterns in reading, beliefs of teachers)? How will these issues be addressed?
   • What levels of approval will be needed to implement your plan? List all the individuals who will need to be contacted regarding this proposal, if it is to succeed.
   • How will you arrange your plan so that the proposed changes provide an extra resource for dealing with difficult-to-teach students and are not simply viewed as an add-on by school personnel?
   • How will the change plan build on current strengths within your school?

5. Describe what will be done to get ready for implementing your plan, considering issues that arose based on your systems analysis, including:

   • How (when, and by whom) will the plan be presented to faculty, parents, and other stakeholders?
   • How will changes be incorporated into the plan?
   • What are anticipated professional development needs of the faculty, and how and when will they be addressed?
   • How and when will teacher planning time be provided to prepare for the implementation of the proposed inclusive school?

6. Describe a framework for ongoing monitoring and evaluation of the inclusive school. Such a plan should address, at a minimum, the academic and social progress made by students with and without disabilities, and teacher, parent, and administration satisfaction with the inclusive school.

hallmark of a good plan at this stage is that it is *flexible* and that planning team members and others who were involved in developing the plan are open to change based on input from the faculty at large. This flexibility will signal to members of the school community that their concerns are taken seriously and that necessary changes will be incorporated into the plan to ensure that these needs are addressed. Furthermore, changes that are made on the basis of suggestions from individuals who were not involved in developing the plan will form a foundation for trust and begin the process of ensuring that the plan is "owned" by a large portion of the school community.

Step 7. Incorporate Feedback from the School Community

This stage will vary, depending on the level of support the inclusion plan receives from the faculty. As noted previously, the more stakeholders are involved in each of the preceding steps, the greater the likelihood that the inclusion plan will be accepted by the school community with only minor changes.

After the necessary changes are made in the plan for inclusion, it should be taken to the school community for final approval. If major concerns arise, it may be necessary to delay implementation or to implement the program on a limited scale (e.g., only with certain teams in a middle school or only at the primary grade level in an elementary school).

Step 8. Get Ready

Once the plan is approved in principle by a majority of the staff, nuts-and-bolts planning should begin in earnest. At this point, teachers should know who will be working together and the type of planning and preparation they will need before the program begins. The major need of teachers at this point is *time* for collaborative planning and to attend needed professional development activities.

As planning for inclusion proceeds, we have found that it is best to develop plans around groups of teachers who will work together or be responsible for a group of students, such as departments in a high school, teams in a middle school, or 4th grade teachers in an elementary school, along with the special education personnel with whom they will collaborate. For example, a team of teachers in a middle school responsible for the education of 120 students—including scheduling the school day and determining blocks of time that are used for various subjects—should work with a special education teacher to make decisions and plan how inclusion will work on their team. This suggests that many models for inclusion may exist, as different teams, grade levels, or departments may handle inclusion differently, depending on the teaching strengths, resources, and preferences of a group of teachers who are collaborating.

One caution at this point is important to note. As nuts-and-bolts plans are being made, it will become obvious that the individual who will be placed in the most demanding position is the special education teacher. This person will lose his or her classroom and students and will be required to work with a range of teachers, fit into their classrooms, and learn their curriculums, instructional styles, classroom discipline preferences, and so forth. One of the major complaints we have heard from inclusive schools is that, all too often, the role of the special education teacher is too disjointed, and the teacher lacks any sense of professional identity and connection with a group of students. In some cases, the special education teacher serves in a professional role that is not in keeping with her skills and professional preparation—a position that leads the special education teacher to feel that she is serving in the role of an instructional assistant. While it must be recognized that, under the best of circumstances, the role of the special education teacher will be a difficult one, it is critical that teachers who are collaborating with the special education teacher be sensitive to these issues and recognize the need to provide a reasonable professional role for the special education teacher.

Step 9. Implement the Plan

One thing we have learned from working with many inclusive schools is that the plan never goes quite as expected. Consider the following example, as described by an elementary school special education teacher:

We spent an entire year getting ready for our inclusion program. I was working with an intermediate team of teachers. We were going to have all our classrooms close together, in one section of the building. We had worked out a schedule, plans for collaborating, methods for adapting instruction, curriculum, expectations, grading. We felt as though we were ready for anything and were so excited about beginning the program. On the inservice day before school began, the principal met with us and said that many more students had enrolled in our school than we expected, and that he was going to have to change schedules, teaching assignments, add teachers, move classrooms around. We were devastated. All our planning went up in smoke!

Admittedly, this example is the most extreme we have seen. Nonetheless, invariably some issue will arise that results in changes to the original plan. A work-in-progress is certainly an apt description of most inclusive schools. Approximately four months after the plans "went up in smoke" for the teachers in the school just described, one of the authors met with the core planning team for this and several other schools that had also recently implemented inclusive programs. Several of the team members complained about putting so much time into planning their program and having to make many changes as the school year began. The author suggested that perhaps this meant that they didn't need so much time to plan the program, as it was going to have to be changed anyway. A chorus of responses arose from the teams objecting to this suggestion. The overwhelming consensus was that they never could have dealt with the changes that were required if not for the planning time they had. This time provided them with the opportunity to explore options for their program (some of which they ended up implementing in short order), to learn to work together as a team and solve problems, and, in general, to gain the confidence they needed to think on their feet and make changes in the inclusive program.

Implementing an inclusive school is never an easy time. Two key issues we take from the experiences described here are

1. Participants in an inclusive school must view the program as a flexible work-in-progress that will be adapted when participants realize something isn't working.

2. Participants need continuing common planning time to address both expected (e.g., planning for coteaching) and unexpected issues that arise.

Step 10. Monitor, Evaluate, and Change as Needed

Much of the rationale for Step 10 was provided in Step 9. However, the critical issue that was not addressed related to the evaluation of the inclusive school. If teachers, administrators, school board members, parents, and other stakeholders are to continue to support inclusive schools, these programs must be demonstrated as effective. This effectiveness should address, at a minimum, three crucial issues:

1. Do students with disabilities benefit from the inclusive school program academically and socially?

2. Do students who are not labeled with disabilities benefit academically and socially from the inclusive school?

3. Do teachers support the inclusive program (that is, do they feel that they have the necessary support to provide a quality education to students who enter their classrooms)?

Many more issues can be addressed when evaluating the inclusive school, including the perspectives of students and parents regarding these programs. As research has demonstrated, well-developed inclusive schools fare well on these evaluation criteria. In contrast, inclusive schools that are poorly developed will lack the support of most teachers, parents, and students, and will also fail to produce academic and social benefits for students.

Lessons Learned

As we look back over our work with local schools, one of the most surprising things is how little we knew about developing inclusive programs when we began. Indeed, we have learned many lessons over the past 10 years. Five lessons, in particular, are key in the development of inclusive programs. Some aspects of these lessons reiterate information provided in previous chapters, and others go beyond what was previously stated.

Lesson 1. Inclusion Begins with Influential Voices

Ten years ago, we began working with two special education administrators in Indiana, one an older male administrator who was nearing retirement, the other a younger female who had just begun her administrative career. These administrators could not have differed more in many ways. One was conservative, traditional, and steeped in the "old boy" network of the state; many thought he would never change his good but very traditional special education programs. The other was a progressive newcomer who bucked trends and was determined to change the face of practice in her schools. In spite of these differences, both of these administrators came to the realization that their special education programs were not working very well and needed to be changed. Students with disabilities in both these districts received much of their education in separate settings, segregated from their typical peers. These students had very little access to the general education curriculum. Many of them were bused far away from their neighborhood schools for special education services. Previous attempts to significantly change these settings had not been successful. Teachers, parents, and administrators in both settings were generally pleased with the services that were provided for students with disabilities. In spite of the barriers, both of these administrators were determined to improve the education of students with disabilities in their local schools. Moreover, both became convinced that this goal could be achieved only if general education classrooms were changed significantly to better accommodate the needs of *all* students, including those with disabilities.

Over the ensuing 10 years, we worked extensively with both of these administrators to develop, implement, and maintain inclusive programs in their schools. We learned many things about leadership and school change from these administrators. Although they differed in their administrative styles, they shared many commonalities in working to change their schools and improve services for students with disabilities, including the following:

• *Both initially sought out allies who supported their vision.* They realized that they could not mandate change and that they needed others to take on leadership roles if the necessary changes were to be realized. They first identified outside experts who believed in inclusion, understood school change, and would work with them in planning change. They then identified principals in local schools who were willing to explore the possibility of developing inclusive programs. These principals subsequently identified influential teachers and other stakeholders in their schools who would take on leadership roles. Thus, leadership was quickly shared by influential proponents of inclusion to ensure that a broad range of professionals shared a common vision and provided leadership for change.

• *Both administrators realized that leadership would require getting out of the way.* While initially both administrators spent much time with the principals and faculties of schools that were considering developing inclusive programs, their work focused on convincing the stakeholders that developing these programs was a good idea and that they would be supported by the central administration in developing these programs. As the meetings progressed, both administrators made it clear that developing the programs was the responsibility of the teachers, administrators, and other stakeholders in the local school. Thus, each local school was empowered to make critical decisions regarding its own inclusive program.

- *Both administrators started small, with one or two schools, and were patient as programs were developed and implemented in these schools over the next one or two years.*
- *Both administrators built on the success of the initial schools by getting other principals and schools to get on board.* At the same time, other stakeholders (parents, school board members, and central office administrators) became supportive of the changes that were being made.

Ten years later, after the retirement of one of these administrators, the development and improvement of inclusive schools in these two school districts continues. Most of the schools in both settings are now inclusive. Both settings have schools that are frequently visited and viewed as models for inclusion. Credit for this success goes to many professionals and other stakeholders who have worked for many years to ensure the success of the programs. However, all this change was made possible by the voices of two influential administrators, who provided strong, positive leadership as inclusive programs were developed and who recognized the need to cultivate other influential leaders who would help them achieve their goal. Of course, this type of leadership can come from many sources, not just directors of special education programs. However, no matter who takes on the leadership role, if successful inclusive programs are to be developed, it is necessary to build a broad base of leadership among persons in different roles in schools and central administration.

Lesson 2. Big Changes in Schools Are Required

This book began with examples of two attempts to develop inclusive programs. One example was of an "add-on" inclusive program, which was implemented with few changes to the school at large. The second example was of a high school that significantly changed practices to develop an inclusive program. We continue to see all too many examples of what are called "inclusive" programs, with very few changes in the overall school. As stated earlier, it is not possible to develop good, successful inclusive programs unless *many, significant* changes are made in the school. If students with disabilities are to have a rhythm of the day that is similar to that of other students; if general education classrooms are to accommodate a broad range of student differences (i.e., difference becomes ordinary); and if teachers are to receive the support they need to meet student needs, significant changes must occur in schools. Teachers must share responsibility for all students in the school and must take on new, collaborative roles to do this. Curriculum and instruction must be examined and changed. The organization of the school day must be changed. In short, every aspect of the school must be examined and, if necessary, changed to ensure that inclusive programs are successful. Short of such changes, schools simply are not organized to accommodate the diverse range of students who enter classrooms, nor are resources available to accommodate this diversity. In short, the work of teachers significantly changes in inclusive schools; what teachers do from hour to hour and day to day changes.

We are often asked, "Is our school really inclusive?" To respond to this question, we often look at the extent to which significant changes have occurred in the school. For example, as the program was developed, did significant changes occur in the following?

- Curriculum (e.g., adaptations in curriculum to meet the needs of all students).
- Instructional methods (e.g., more explicit instruction).
- Classroom organization (e.g., students working together more often).
- School organization (e.g., schedule of the school day is changed).
- Teacher and administrator beliefs about teaching and learning (e.g., curriculum should be adapted to meet the needs of students rather than expecting students to march through a set curriculum).

In addition to looking at how these five aspects of the school have changed, we attempt to determine if the rhythm of the day for students with disabilities is similar to that of other students and if *dif-*

ference is an ordinary part of the inclusive classroom. Although our standards are high for recognizing a school as inclusive, we feel that these changes are absolutely necessary if a successful program is to be developed. Stakeholders must recognize how much change must occur and how pervasive the changes will be. Moreover, we have found that developing an inclusive program is always harder than stakeholders initially think it will be. Indeed, successful programs are dynamic and ever-changing, presenting continuing challenges to teachers and administrators as they create classrooms to meet a broad range of student needs. As one teacher said,

EXAMPLE

One of the things I like the most, and dislike the most, about my classroom is how I have to always be thinking about the students and what they need. It used to be that I could teach a science lesson that I had taught 20 times before and put my mind on automatic pilot. The lesson would just flow, the way it always did. Now, I always have to think about what I'm doing, look at what students need to learn, what they are learning, whether I'm missing some students. Most of the time, I like this new approach to teaching: it's challenging, stimulating. However, to be honest, at times it puts quite a strain on me. I'd like to be able to put it on automatic pilot and not have to think so much about what I'm doing. One thing I will say, in my [inclusive] classroom, there is never a dull moment!

Lesson 3. Schools Change in Many Ways, Both Expected and Unexpected

As noted previously, implementing inclusive programs changes schools in many ways, both expected and unexpected. At the most basic level, classrooms improve as they become more accommodating of student needs. Teachers learn from one another and become better teachers. The "differences" that exist among students in classrooms become an ordinary part of the classroom, rather than deviations from the "norm." As every teacher knows, all students differ from the norm, at least on occasion. For example, all students have at least an occasional need for extra support in learning academic material or getting along with other students in the classroom. Thus, the changes that occur in inclusive classrooms benefit *all* students in a variety of ways, as all students are more readily accommodated as part of the learning and social community of the classroom.

In addition to these obvious benefits, inclusive programs improve classrooms and schools in ways that at times are unexpected and difficult to measure. One of the most important of these benefits occurs when learning communities develop in classrooms, in which students often work together and provide one another with assistance in developing academic skills or making friends. These learning communities, as well as other aspects of inclusive programs, affect students' attitudes toward one another in many positive ways. For example, as one principal told us,

EXAMPLE

The kids in our school get along better than they used to [before the inclusive program]. I especially notice it on the playground, where students don't fight as much, and we are a lot less likely to hear racial slurs. I don't mean to suggest that we don't have any problems. We still have some students who are mean to other people. But even in those cases, other students will come to the aid of their friends, or teachers are more attentive to conflicts and put-downs. I think if you talked to our students you'd find that our school is just a better place to be now, more supportive of them, more fun, whether they are in the classroom, on the playground, in the cafeteria, or in the restroom. They feel more comfortable . . . and safe in our school.

Lesson 4. Inclusive Isn't Just About Special Education

As the previous lessons illustrate, inclusion isn't just about special education or students with disabilities. Moreover, what is entailed in developing these programs are deliberations regarding how schools are improved and general education classrooms become more

142

accommodating for *all* students. For example, one of the most frequent questions we hear as we initially discuss inclusive programs with a school faculty is how these concepts relate to students with gifts and talents. Actually, this information doesn't often take the form of a question; more often, one or more teachers will point out that many of the concepts that we discuss when describing inclusion are important for students with gifts and talents. These teachers often go on to note that these students frequently do not fit into general education classrooms and may cause disturbances because they are bored by classroom work and expectations that do not meet their needs. Indeed, it is easy to make the case that one of the primary focuses of inclusive programs ought to be on developing general education classrooms that are more accommodating for and supportive of students with gifts and talents. The same could be said for any number of other "groups" of students, including those who learn the academic content of the classroom more slowly than others but who are not identified with a disability, students who are more active than the typical student, students who are inattentive, students who have difficulty getting along with others, students who are English language learners, and many other students who may or may not fit neatly into a category. Inclusion becomes the same as school improvement rather than a school change endeavor that focuses on students with disabilities.

We gained insight into this issue a few years ago while searching for principals of local schools who might be interested in working to develop inclusive programs:

EXAMPLE

Several years ago we participated in a project to support teachers and administrators as they developed or improved inclusive programs in their schools. We were searching for schools that were interested in working with us during the final year of this project. We discussed the project with a local director of special education, and he agreed to talk with the elementary principals in his district. We later heard from

—continued—

—continued—

EXAMPLE

the local director that the principals were not interested in participating in the project, as they felt their inclusive programs worked relatively well and they had many needs that took priority over further developing these programs. A month or so later, one of these principals called us and said that she and some of her colleagues had heard about a "school improvement" project we were working on with schools in a nearby district. (This was the same project that was previously characterized as an "inclusion" project.) This principal had heard about the project from a teacher in one of the schools, who described the project to her. As they continued to talk, this principal made it clear that she viewed "inclusion" as something that addressed only the needs of students with disabilities and that she was not interested in such a limited program. On the other hand, she and several of her peers in local schools were quite interested in an opportunity to work with a team from their schools in developing a plan to make their school more accommodating for all students (i.e., not inclusion, but more general school improvement). We realized that words were getting in the way. The project had been described as an inclusion initiative, but this principal viewed what we were doing as general school improvement. We went on to work with four of the best inclusive schools in this district to develop and implement school improvement plans designed to make their schools more accommodating for all students.

We learned a great deal from this experience. For one thing, many principals had little interest in taking on a major initiative to change their school if the initiative promised to provide direct help for only 10–15 percent of their population (i.e., students with disabilities). On the other hand, many principals *were* interested if the initiative promised to address the needs of most students in their schools. Furthermore, at least in this school district, "inclusion" had become a shorthand way of conveying that only the needs of students with disabilities would be addressed, while "school improvement" would address the needs of all students. Obviously, the use of these terms will vary from district to district and state to state. Nonetheless, the lesson learned from this experience will stay with us. An inclusive program, school improvement, or whatever it is called is much more likely to be undertaken if the activity entails examining the school and developing a program that addresses the needs of a broad range of students in the school rather than just students with disabilities. Indeed, the development of inclusive programs must become synonymous with school improvement if the necessary changes are to occur that ensure that high-quality inclusive programs are developed.

Lesson 5. How People Feel and Think Is Most Important

People put off or do not develop inclusive programs for many reasons. They are very difficult to develop. Many stressful changes in school practices are required. The changes are never-ending, and teachers must remain ever-vigilant to ensure that the program is working. School districts often have limited resources and claim not to have enough money to develop a "good" inclusive program. Class sizes are too large. There aren't enough special education teachers to develop a good program. Many students with disabilities can't pass tests that are required to move from one grade level to the next. Many students with disabilities can't pass gateway tests that are required to graduate from high school. Inclusion may negatively affect the education of students who are not identified with disabilities. Low test scores of students with disabilities may reflect negatively on a local school. Students with disabilities may take too much of the classroom teacher's time. Students with disabilities may disrupt the regular classroom routine. Some (perhaps many) students with disabilities can't do the work that is required in the general education classroom.

There could be many other objections, but the point is clear. There are literally hundreds of reasons not to develop inclusive programs. All of these reasons contain at least a grain of truth (and sometimes much more than a grain). There is no doubt that inclusive programs are difficult to develop. Indeed, all the barriers that

teachers and administrators must overcome to develop these programs make us wonder at times why so many programs are being
developed across the United States (McLeskey, Henry, & Hodges,
1998; McLeskey & Henry, 1999).

The bottom line is that people develop inclusive programs
because they decide it is important to develop these programs. As
Biklen (1985) so aptly stated several years ago, the development of
inclusive programs "HAS MORE TO DO WITH HOW PEOPLE FEEL
and THINK THAN ANYTHING ELSE" (p. 60, caps in original). If
teachers and administrators in a local school decide that it is important that an inclusive program be developed, they will develop a
program. Perhaps a "better" program could be developed if class
sizes were reduced, more resources were made available, or other
barriers did not exist. But these barriers do not stand in the way of
professionals who have decided to develop an inclusive program.
They find ways to efficiently use resources and to create additional
resources (for example, by having students support one another at
times) when necessary. They develop a program that uses resources
equitably to meet the needs of *all* students in the school. In short,
they develop the best program they can, with the resources that are
available, based on the belief that inclusive programs are in the best
interests of *all* students.

Appendix:
Resources for Developing
Inclusive Schools

General Textbooks

The textbooks reviewed here present a broad range of topics and issues to consider when developing inclusive schools and classrooms. While the presentation of some strategies and issues may be elementary for experienced teachers, all educators may benefit from their application and discussion within the context of inclusion, improving instruction, and meeting the diverse learning needs of a broad range of students.

Friend, M., & Bursuck, W. D. (1999). *Including students with special needs: A practical guide for classroom teachers* (2nd ed.). Needham Heights, MA: Allyn and Bacon.

This book offers teaching strategies for students with low-incidence and high-incidence disabilities at both the elementary and secondary levels. The authors discuss foundational issues related to special education and inclusion and review numerous classroom strategies in the context of specific classroom situations. This book is particularly useful for experienced educators who would like a quick review of foundational knowledge and further information on implementation of strategies in an inclusive framework. Selected topics of interest are

- Analyzing classroom and student needs.
- Instructional adaptations.
- Learning strategies.
- Evaluating student learning.

- Responding to student behavior.
- Building social relationships.

Salend, S. J. (1998). *Effective mainstreaming: Creating inclusive classrooms* (3rd ed.). Upper Saddle River, NJ: Prentice-Hall, Inc.

This text emphasizes developing an inclusive classroom that meets the needs of all students, regardless of disability, gender, socioeconomic status, family structure, ethnicity, or linguistic background. Student diversity in inclusive classrooms is presented and discussed in the context of effective classroom settings, practices, and instructional strategies. Topics included are

- Promoting communication and collaboration.
- Facilitating acceptance of individual differences and friendships.
- Helping students make transitions to inclusive settings.
- Modifying instruction for diverse learners.
- Adapting large- and small-group instruction.

Vaughn, S., Bos, C. S., & Schumm, J. S. (2000). *Teaching exceptional, diverse, and at-risk students in the general education classroom* (2nd ed.). Needham Heights, MA: Allyn and Bacon.

This textbook provides educators with the knowledge base, tools, and practical strategies to accommodate a broad range of student needs in an inclusive classroom. It provides a framework for adaptation, along with an emphasis on learning activities and sample lessons that address both elementary and secondary classrooms. Extensive information on curriculum adaptation is appropriate to educators across various levels of experience, addressing strategies and activities for teaching reading, writing, mathematics, and content areas. This text is an excellent resource on the following topics:

- Planning and grouping strategies.
- Facilitating reading.
- Facilitating writing.
- Helping students succeed in mathematics.
- Teaching in the content areas.
- Managing student behavior.
- Promoting social acceptance.

Inclusion, School Change, and Collaboration

This set of resources addresses the general topics of inclusion, school change, and collaboration. While most focus specifically on inclusion—emphasizing philosophy, attitudes, or program development—other sources focus on critical skills that are often a foundation to inclusive programs, such as collaboration.

Friend, M., & Cook, L. (1996). *Interactions: Collaboration skills for school professionals* (2nd ed.). White Plains, NY: Longman.

This book describes a skills-based approach to communication and collaboration as a means of improving interactions among educators. It covers a range of topics that provide a knowledge base and discussion of issues that address collaborative practices in schools and interpersonal work relationships. The material in this resource is appropriate for experienced educators and for those interested in developing or improving inclusive educational options in schools. Relevant topics include:

- Fundamentals of collaboration.
- Interpersonal communication and problem solving.
- Understanding conflict.
- Applications to coteaching and staff development.

Stainback, S., & Stainback, W. (1996). *Inclusion: A guide for educators*. Baltimore: Brookes Publishing.

This book includes chapters from a range of education experts on the tools and techniques needed to support inclusion in the classroom. Topical areas with multiple chapters include curriculum, collaboration, behavior, teaching methods, and administrative issues.

Villa, R. A., & Thousand, J. S. (Eds.). (1995). *Creating an inclusive school*. Alexandria, VA: Association for Supervision and Curriculum Development.

This book provides discussion of the philosophical and legal foundations of inclusion, in addition to information about curriculum and school change. Personal perspectives are provided through stories by teachers and parents of students participating in inclusive classrooms, as well as reflections of an adult with a disability.

Walther-Thomas, C., Korinek, L., McLaughlin, V., & Williams, B. T. (2000). *Collaboration for inclusive education: Developing successful programs.* Needham Heights, MA: Allyn and Bacon.

The authors address the topic of collaboration as a critical cornerstone in developing inclusive schools and classrooms. Issues, examples, and skill-building activities are presented to assist educators in developing the necessary knowledge, skills, and attitudes that will promote inclusive education. A strength of this resource is the authors' emphasis on addressing issues and topics from multiple levels: classroom, school, and district. Relevant topics include:

- Essential features of inclusive programs.
- Collaborative support networks for professionals and students.
- Collaborative consultation.
- Coteaching.

Instruction and Curriculum: Adaptation, Differentiation, and Constructivist Views

This set of resources covers a broad range of topics on curriculum and instruction. Varying approaches are explained that serve to enrich and change the learning environment to meet the needs of a diverse range of students in an inclusive classroom. These approaches range from those requiring minimal change (adaptation of the core curriculum) to others that require substantial change in curriculum and instructional approaches (differentiation of instruction, constructivist learning).

Armstrong, T. (2000). *Multiple intelligences in the classroom* (2nd ed.). Alexandria, VA: Association for Supervision and Curriculum Development.

After introducing the theory of multiple intelligences, the author applies the theory to educational settings and issues, including curriculum development, teaching strategies, thematic planning, assessment, and special education. Numerous classroom examples, sample lessons, and materials are presented.

Brooks, J. G., & Brooks, M. (1993). *In search of understanding: The case for constructivist classrooms*. Alexandria, VA: Association for Supervision and Curriculum Development.

The authors describe the characteristics of constructivism and provide descriptors of constructivist learning environments and teaching approaches. This book is an excellent introduction to constructivist classrooms and how they differ from traditional classroom learning environments.

Deschenes, C., Ebeling, D. G., & Sprague, J. (1994). *Adapting curriculum and instruction in inclusive classrooms: A teacher's desk reference*. Bloomington, IN: Institute for the Study of Developmental Disabilities.

This resource provides a conceptual model and a range of sample adaptations that educators can use with individual students and classrooms. Specific examples are provided of inclusive lessons in reading, language arts, math, social studies, and science, in addition to suggestions for testing and grading. Sample forms also are included.

Kamenuii, E. J., & Simmons, D. C. (1999). *Towards successful inclusion of students with disabilities: The architecture of instruction*. Reston, VA: The Council for Exceptional Children.

This monograph provides an introductory overview of the general principles of adaptation of curricular materials. The authors describe the processes of cognitive ramps and scaffolding, provide principles of effective curriculum design, and apply these concepts to beginning reading and written expression.

Pugach, M. C., & Warger, C. L. (Eds.). (1996). *Curriculum trends, special education, and reform: Refocusing the conversation*. New York: Teachers College Press.

This edited book provides in-depth discussion of current curriculum trends and the interplay of general education and special education reform efforts. The content areas of science, mathematics, social studies, and literacy are explored through the use of multiple examples that emphasize a constructivist approach to curriculum development.

Putnam, J. W. (1998). *Cooperative learning and strategies for inclusion* (2nd ed.). Baltimore: Brookes Publishing.

A comprehensive guide to using cooperative learning in inclusive classrooms. Starting with a strong research foundation, the author presents strategies and techniques to assist teachers in setting up cooperative learning that can enhance the outcomes of inclusion, both for social acceptance of students with disabilities and for the academic achievement of all students. Topics include the process of cooperative learning, curricular and instructional adaptations, multiple intelligences, and conflict management.

Schumaker, J., & Lenz, K. (1999). *Adapting language arts, social studies, and science materials for the inclusive classroom.* Reston, VA: The Council for Exceptional Children.

This monograph focuses on curricular adaptation in grades 3 through 8, in the areas of language arts, science, and social studies. The authors explain content and format adaptations, providing numerous research-supported examples of strategies that could be adopted to make the general education curriculum more accessible to students with mild disabilities. Specific topics include strategy instruction, content organizers, and mnemonic adaptations. Includes numerous examples of adapting existing materials, mediating existing materials, and selecting alternative materials.

Schumm, J. S. (1999). *Adapting reading and math materials for the inclusive classroom.* Reston, VA: The Council for Exceptional Children.

Using the content areas of reading and math, this monograph provides a process of curricular adaptation for K–5th grade. Basic tools for organizing classrooms and providing adaptations are presented in four categories: providing direct assistance, structuring lessons to promote learning from materials, simplifying or supplementing existing materials, and teaching strategies for using materials.

Slavin, R. E. (1995). *Cooperative learning: Theory, research, and practice* (2nd ed.). Needham Heights, MA: Allyn and Bacon.

The author provides a thorough foundation regarding the theory and research addressing cooperative learning. Much of the book focuses on specific cooperative learning strategies such as Student Teams—Achievement Division (STAD), Jigsaw–II, and Teams–Games–Tournaments (TGT), along with issues of team building, grouping students, and group outcomes.

Tomlinson, C. A. (1999). *The differentiated classroom: Responding to the needs of all learners.* Alexandria, VA: Association for Supervision and Curriculum Development.

Through a blend of research and practice examples, the author provides a framework for creating classroom learning environments that support differentiated instruction. Chapters describe individual lessons, units of instruction, and classrooms with differentiated instruction in action across the elementary and secondary levels.

Social Climate: Friendships, Promoting Positive Behaviors, Social Skills

Resources that address the social climate of inclusive schools and classrooms are included in many of the books already reviewed in this appendix. Educators should find the following books and chapters useful in reflecting on and discussing this topic in the process of developing an inclusive school.

Bradley, D., & Graves, D. K. (1997). Student support networks. In D. Bradley, M. King-Sears, & D. Tessier-Switlick (Eds.), *Teaching students in inclusive settings* (pp. 394–403). Needham Heights, MA: Allyn and Bacon.

The authors suggest specific strategies for establishing and maintaining friendships, as well as using noncompetitive games for friendship development.

Cartledge, G., & Milburn, J. F. (1995). *Teaching social skills to children and youth*. Boston: Allyn and Bacon.

The authors focus on the development of prosocial, adaptive skills through an instructional process that uses modeling, role playing, and coaching. Attention is given to the generalization and maintenance of social skills and application to distinct student groups: preschool, adolescents, students with disabilities, and students from culturally diverse backgrounds.

McGinnis, E., & Goldstein, A. P. (1997). *Skillstreaming the elementary school child* (rev. ed.). Champaign, IL: Research Press.

This book presents an often-used social skills curriculum and suggested grouping and instructional techniques that can be used in inclusive classrooms. ˙

Putnam, J. W. (1998). *Cooperative learning and strategies for inclusion* (2nd ed.). Baltimore: Brookes Publishing.

Topics include interpersonal relationships, peer acceptance, developing cooperative and social skills, appreciating diversity, and conflict resolution.

Stainback, S., & Stainback, W. (1996). *Inclusion: A guide for educators*. Baltimore: Brookes Publishing.

Topics include facilitating friendships, student collaboration, caring communities, preventing disruptive behavior, and promoting positive behavior.

References

Aronson, E., Blaney, N., Stephan, C., Sikes, J., & Snapp, M. (1978). *The jigsaw classroom.* Beverly Hills, CA: Sage.

Baines, L., Baines, C., & Masterson, C. (1994). Mainstreaming: One school's reality. *Phi Delta Kappan, 76*(1), 39–40, 57–64.

Barnes, E., Berrigan, C., & Biklen, D. (1978). *What's the difference? Teaching positive attitudes toward people with disabilities.* Syracuse, NY: Human Policy Press.

Biklen, D. (1985). *Achieving the complete school: Strategies for effective mainstreaming.* New York: Teachers College Press.

Biklen, D. (1989). Making difference ordinary: Strategies for educating students with varying abilities together. In S. Stainback & W. Stainback (Eds.). *Educating all students in regular education* (pp. 235–248). Baltimore: Brookes.

Blackorby, J., & Wagner, M. (1996). Longitudinal postschool outcomes of youth with disabilities: Findings from the National Longitudinal Transition Study. *Exceptional Children, 62,* 399–413.

Brooks, J. G., & Brooks, M. (1993). *In search of understanding: The case for constructivist classrooms.* Alexandria, VA: Association for Supervision and Curriculum Development.

Bull, B., & Buechler, B. (1997). *Planning together: Professional development for teachers of ALL students.* Bloomington, IN: Indiana Education Policy Center.

Burrello, L., Lashley, C., & Van Dyke, R. (1996). Aligning job accountability standards in a unified system of education. *The Special Education Leadership Review, 3*(1), 29–41.

Canady, R., & Rettig, M. (1993, December). Unlocking the lockstep high school schedule. *Phi Delta Kappan, 75,* 310–314.

Carnegie Council on Adolescent Development (1989). Turning points: Preparing American youth for the 21st century. New York: Author.

Carpenter, S., & McKee-Higgins, E. (1998). Behavior management in inclusive classrooms. In E. Meyen, G. Vergason, & E. Whelan (Eds.).

Educating students with mild disabilities (pp. 115–129). Denver, CO: Love Publishing.

Cartledge, G., & Johnson, C. (1996). Inclusive classrooms for students with emotional and behavioral disorders: Critical variables. *Theory into Practice, 35*(1), 51–57.

Cegelka, P., & Tyler, J. (1970). The efficacy of special class placement for mentally retarded in proper perspective. *Training School Bulletin, 67*(1), 33–67.

Charles, C. M. (1996). *Building classroom discipline* (5th ed.). White Plains, NY: Longman.

Clay, M. M. (1985). *The early detection of reading difficulties* (3rd ed.). Auckland, NZ: Heineman.

Cole, C. (1995). *A contextualized understanding of teachers' practice, their collaborative relationships, and the inclusion of students with disabilities.* Unpublished doctoral dissertation (AAC9601781). Indiana University, Bloomington.

Cole, C., & McLeskey, J. (1997, February). Secondary inclusion programs for students with mild disabilities. *Focus on Exceptional Children, 29,* 1–15.

Cullinan, D., Sabornie, E., & Crossland, C. (1992). Social mainstreaming of mildly handicapped students. *Elementary School Journal, 92*(3), 339–351.

Deci, E., & Ryan, R. (1985). *Intrinsic motivation and self-determination in human behavior.* New York: Plenum.

Delquadri, J., Greenwood, C., Whorton, D., Carta, J., & Hall, V. (1986). Classwide peer tutoring. *Exceptional Children, 52*(6), 535–542.

Deschenes, C., Ebeling, D., & Sprague, J. (1994). Adapting curriculum & instruction in inclusive classrooms: A teacher's desk reference. Bloomington, IN: Institute for the Study of Developmental Disabilities.

Deshler, D., Ellis, E., & Lenz, K. (1996). *Teaching adolescents with learning disabilities: Strategies and methods* (2nd ed.). Denver, CO: Love Publishing.

Deshler, D., & Schumaker, J. (1988). Implementing the regular education initiative in secondary schools: A different ball game. *Journal of Learning Disabilities, 21*(1), 36–42.

Dunn, L. (1968). Special education for the mildly retarded—is much of it justifiable? *Exceptional Children, 35*(1), 3–22.

Ellis, E. (1993). Integrative strategy instruction: A potential model for teaching content area subjects to adolescents with learning disabilities. *Journal of Learning Disabilities, 26*(1), 358–363.

Emmer, E., Evertson, C., Clements, B., & Worsham, M. (1997). *Classroom management for secondary teachers* (4th ed.). Boston: Allyn & Bacon.

Falvey, M. A. (Ed.) (1995). *Inclusive and heterogeneous schooling.* Baltimore: Brookes.

Falvey, M. A., & Rosenberg, R. (1995). Developing and fostering friendships. In M. A. Falvey (Ed.). *Inclusive and heterogeneous schooling* (pp. 267–283). Baltimore: Brookes.

Ferguson, D. (1995). The real challenge of inclusion. *Phi Delta Kappan, 77*(4), 281–287.

Ferguson, D., Meyer, G., Jeanchild, L., Juniper, L., & Zingo, J. (1992). Figuring out what to do with the grownups: How teachers make inclusion "work" for students with disabilities. *Journal for the Association of Persons with Severe Handicaps, 17*(4), 218–226.

Fox, N., & Ysseldyke, J. (1997). Implementing inclusion at the middle level: Lessons from a negative example. *Exceptional Children, 64*(1), 81–98.

Friend, M., & Bursuck, B. (1998). *Including students with special needs.* Boston: Allyn & Bacon.

Fuchs, D., Fuchs, L., Harris, A., & Roberts, P. H. (1996). Bridging the research-to-practice gap with mainstreaming assistance teams: A cautionary tale. *School Psychology Quarterly, 11*(3), 244–266.

Fullan, M. (1993). *Change forces.* Bristol, PA: Falmer Press.

Fullan, M., & Miles, M. (1992, June). Getting reform right: What works and what doesn't. *Phi Delta Kappan, 73*, 745–752.

Fullan, M. & Stiegelbauer, S. (1991). *The new meaning of educational change.* New York: Teachers College Press.

Gersten, R., Vaughn, S., Deshler, D., & Schiller, E. (1997). What we know about using research findings: Implications for improving special education practice. *Journal of Learning Disabilities, 30*(5), 466–476.

Gersten, R., Walker, H., & Darch, C. (1988). Relationship between teachers' effectiveness and their tolerance for handicapped students. *Exceptional Children, 54*(5), 433–438.

Giangreco, M., Dennis, R., Cloninger, C., Edelman, S., & Schattman, R. (1993). "I've counted Jon": Transformational experiences of teachers educating students with disabilities. *Exceptional Children, 59*(4), 359–372.

Giangreco, M., Edelman, S., & Dennis, R. (1991). Common professional practices that interfere with the integrated delivery of related services. *Remedial and Special Education, 12*(2), 16–24.

Glasser, W. (1986). *Control theory in the classroom.* New York: Harper & Row.

Goldstein, H., Moss, J., & Jordan, L. (1965). *The efficacy of special class training on the development of mentally retarded children.* Cooperative research project no. 619. Washington, DC: U.S. Office of Education.

Goodman, J. (1995). Change without difference: School restructuring in historical perspective. *Harvard Educational Review, 65*(1), 1–29.

Gould, S. J. (1983). *Hen's teeth and horse's toes.* New York: Norton.

Gritzmacher, H., & Larkin, D. (1993). A comparison of middle level and special education. *Middle School Journal, 25*(1), 28–32.

Hallenbeck, M., & McMaster, D. (1991). Disability simulation for regular education students. *Teaching Exceptional Children, 23*(3), 12–15.

Haynes, M., & Jenkins, J. (1986). Reading instruction in special education resource rooms. *American Educational Research Journal, 23*(2), 161–190.

Jenkins, J., Jewell, M., Leicester, N., O'Connor, R., Jenkins, L., & Troutner, N. (1994). Accommodations for individual differences without classroom ability groups: An experiment in school restructuring. *Exceptional Children, 60*(4), 344–358.

Jenlink, P., Reigeluth, C., Carr, A., & Nelson, L. (1998). Guidelines for facilitating systemic change in school districts. *Systems Research and Behavioral Science, 15*(3), 217–233.

Johnson, D., & Johnson, R. (1991). *Learning together and alone: Cooperative, competitive, and individualistic learning* (3rd ed.). Boston: Allyn and Bacon.

Jorgensen, C. (1998a). Examples of inclusive curriculum units and lessons. In C. Jorgensen (Ed.), *Restructuring high schools for all students: Taking inclusion to the next level* (pp. 107–144). Baltimore: Brookes Publishing.

Jorgensen, C. (Ed.) (1998b). *Restructuring high schools for all students: Taking inclusion to the next level.* Baltimore: Brookes Publishing.

Kauffman, J., Lloyd, J. W., Baker, J., and Riedel, T. M. (1995, March). Inclusion of all students with emotional or behavioral disorders? Let's think again. *Phi Delta Kappan,* 542–546.

Kavale, K., & Forness, S. (1996). Social skills deficits and learning disabilities: A meta-analysis. *Journal of Learning Disabilities, 29*(3), 226–237.

King-Sears, M. (1998). Best academic practices for inclusive classrooms. In E. Meyen, G. Vergason, & E. Whelan (Eds.), *Educating students with mild disabilities* (pp. 305–338). Denver, CO: Love Publishing.

Klausmeier, H. (1975). IGE: An alternative form of schooling. In H. Talmage (Ed.), *Systems of individualized education* (pp. 48–83). Berkeley, CA: McCutchan.

Klingner, J., Vaughn, S., Hughes, M., Schumm, J., & Elbaum, B. (1998). Outcomes for students with and without learning disabilities in inclusive classrooms. *Learning Disabilities Research and Practice, 13*(3), 153–161.

Kohn, A. (1996). *Beyond discipline: From compliance to community.* Alexandria, VA: Association for Supervision and Curriculum Development.

Mathes, P., Fuchs, L., Fuchs, D., Hanley, A., & Sanders, A. (1994). Increasing strategic reading practice with Peabody Classwide Peer Tutoring. *Learning Disabilities Research and Practice, 9*(1), 44–48.

McGill-Franzen, A., & Allington, R. (1991). The gridlock of low reading achievement: Perspectives on practice and policy, *Remedial and Special Education, 12*(3), 20–30.

McGookey, K. (1992). Drama, disability, and your classroom. *Teaching Exceptional Children, 24*(2), 12–14.

McLeskey, J., & Henry, D. (1999). Inclusion: What progress is being made across states? *Teaching Exceptional Children, 31*(5), 56–62.

McLeskey, J., Henry, D., & Hodges, D. (1998). Inclusion: Where is it happening? *Teaching Exceptional Children, 31*(1), 4–11.

McLeskey, J., Skiba, R., & Wilcox, B. (1990). Reform and special education: A mainstream perspective. *Journal of Special Education, 24*(3), 319–325.

McLeskey, J., & Waldron, N. L. (1996). Responses to questions teachers and administrators frequently ask about inclusion. *Phi Delta Kappan, 78*(2), 150–156.

Mikulecky, L., Albers, P., & Peers, M. (1994). *Literacy transfer: A review of the literature* (Technical report TR 94-05). Philadelphia: University of Pennsylvania, National Center on Adult Literacy.

Mikulecky, L., & Lloyd, P. (1993). *The impact of workplace literacy programs: A new model for evaluating the impact of workplace literacy programs.* (Technical report TR 93-2). Philadelphia: University of Pennsylvania, National Center on Adult Literacy.

Nolan, J., & Francis, P. (1992). Changing perspectives in curriculum and instruction. In C. D. Glickman (Ed.), *Supervision in transition (1992 Yearbook of the Association for Supervision and Curriculum Development)* (pp. 44–60). Alexandria, VA: Association for Supervision and Curriculum Development.

Pinnell, G., Short, A., Lyons, C., & Young, P. (1986). *The reading recovery project in Columbus, Ohio. Year 1: 1985–1986.* Columbus, OH: Ohio State University.

Polloway, E., Patton, J., Epstein, M., & Smith, T. (1993). Comprehensive curriculum for students with mild disabilities. In E. Meyen, G. Vergason, & E. Whelan (Eds.), *Educating students with mild disabilities* (pp. 255–272). Denver, CO: Love Publishing.

Poplin, M., & Stone, A. (1992). Paradigm shifts in instructional strategies. From reductionism to holistic/constructivism. In W. Stainback & S. Stainback (Eds.), *Controversial issues confronting special education: Divergent perspectives* (pp. 153–180). Boston: Allyn and Bacon.

Pugach, M. (1995). On the failure of imagination in inclusive schooling. *The Journal of Special Education, 29*(2), 212–223.

Pugach, M., & Warger, C. (1993). Curriculum considerations. In John I. Goodlad and Thomas C. Lovitt (Eds.), *Integrating general and special education* (pp. 125–148). New York: Macmillan.

Pugach, M., & Warger, C. (Eds.). (1996). *Curriculum trends, special education, and reform.* New York: Teachers College Press.

Rieth, H., & Polsgrove, L. (1994). Curriculum and instructional issues in teaching secondary students with learning disabilities. *Learning Disabilities Research & Practice, 9*(2), 118–126.

Rieth, H., & Polsgrove, L. (1998). Curriculum and instructional issues in teaching secondary students with learning disabilities. In E. Meyen, G. Vergason, & E. Whelan (Eds.), *Educating students with mild disabilities* (pp. 255–273). Denver, CO: Love Publishing.

Roach, V. (1995, December). Supporting inclusion: Beyond the rhetoric. *Phi Delta Kappan, 77,* 295–299.

Sailor, W. (1991). Special education in the restructured school. *Remedial and Special Education, 12*(6), 8–22.

Sale, P., & Carey, D. (1995). The sociometric status of students with disabilities in a full-inclusion school. *Exceptional Children, 62*(1), 6–19.

Salend, S. (1998). *Effective mainstreaming: Creating inclusive classrooms.* Columbus, OH: Merrill.

Sarason, S. (1990). *The predictable failure of educational reform.* San Francisco: Jossey-Bass Publishers.

Sarason, S. (1995). *School change: The personal development of a point of view.* New York: Teachers College Press.

Scanlon, D., Deshler, D., & Schumaker, J. (1996). Can a strategy be taught and learned in secondary inclusive classrooms? *Learning Disabilities Research and Practice, 11*(1), 41–57.

Schrumpf, F. (1994). The role of students resolving conflicts in schools. In J. Thousand, R. Villa, & A. Nevin (Eds.), *Creativity and collaborative learning: A practical guide to empowering students and teachers* (pp. 275–292). Baltimore: Brookes.

Schumaker, J., & Deshler, D. (1988). Implementing the regular education initiative in secondary schools: A different ball game. *Journal of Learning Disabilities, 21*(1), 36–42.

Schumaker, J., Deshler, D., & Ellis, E. (1986). Intervention issues related to the education of LD adolescents. In J. K. Torgeson & B. Y. L. Wong (Eds.), *Psychological and educational perspectives on learning disabilities* (pp. 329–365). Orlando, FL: Academic Press.

Schwartz, S. (1991). *Exceptional people: A guide for understanding.* New York: McGraw-Hill.

Scott, B., Vitale, M., & Masten, W. (1998). Implementing instructional adaptations for students with disabilities in inclusive classrooms: A literature review. *Remedial and Special Education, 19*(2), 106–119.

Scruggs, T., & Mastropieri, M. (1996). Teacher perceptions of mainstreaming/inclusion, 1958–1995: A research synthesis. *Exceptional Children, 63*(1), 59–74.

Shanker, A. (1994, December/1995, January). Full inclusion is neither free nor appropriate. *Educational Leadership, 52*(4), 18–21.

Slavin, R. (1994). *Cooperative learning* (2nd ed.). Boston: Allyn & Bacon.

Slavin, R. (1997). Including inclusion in school reform: Success for all and roots and wings. In D. Lipsky & A. Gartner (Eds.), *Inclusion and school reform* (pp. 375–387). Baltimore: Brookes.

Slavin, R., Madden, N., Dolan, L., Wasik, B., Ross, S., & Smith, L. (1994, April). "Whenever and wherever we choose": The replication of Success for All. *Phi Delta Kappan, 75,* 639–647.

Smith, S. (1990). Individualized education programs (IEPs) in special education—From intent to acquiescence. *Exceptional Children, 57*(1), 6–14.

Smith, T. E. C., Polloway, E., Patton, J. R., & Dowdy, C. A. (1998). *Teaching students with special needs in inclusive settings* (2nd ed.). Boston: Allyn & Bacon.

Smith, D., & Rivera, D. (1998). Discipline in special education and general education settings. In Meyen, E., G. Vergason, & E. Whelan (Eds.), *Educating students with mild disabilities* (2nd ed.) (pp. 5–26). Denver, CO: Love Publishing.

Snell, M. (1990). Schools are for all kids: The importance of integration for students with severe disabilities and their peers. In J. W. Lloyd, A. C. Repp, & N. N. Singh (Eds.), *The regular education initiative: Alternative perspectives on concepts, issues, and models* (pp. 225–239). Sycamore, IL: Sycamore Press.

Snow, J., & Forest, M. (1987). Circles. In M. Forest (Ed.), *More education integration: A further collection of reading on the integration of children with mental handicaps into regular school systems* (pp. 169–176). Downsview, Ontario: G. Allan Roeher Institute.

Spear-Swerling, L., & Sternberg, R. (1996). *Off track: When poor readers become "learning disabled."* Boulder, CO: Westview Press.

Stainback, S., Stainback, W., & Jackson, H. (1992). Toward inclusive classrooms. In S. Stainback & W. Stainback (Eds.), *Curriculum considerations in inclusive classrooms: Facilitating learning for all students* (pp. 3–17). Baltimore: Brookes.

Stainback, W., Stainback, S., & Wilkinson, A. (1992). Encouraging peer support and friendships. *Teaching Exceptional Children, 24*(2), 6–11.

Sugai, G., & Lewis, T. (1998). Preferred and promising practices for social skill instruction. In E. Meyen, G. Vergason, & E. Whelan (Eds.), *Educating students with mild disabilities* (2nd ed.) (pp. 137–162). Denver, CO: Love Publishing.

Szymanski, E., & Parker, R. (1989). Supported employment in rehabilitation counseling: Issues and practices. *Journal of Applied Rehabilitation Counseling, 20* (3), 65–72.

Tindal, G., & Marston, D. (1990). *Classroom-based assessment: Evaluating instructional outcomes.* New York: Merrill.

Tomlinson, C. A. (1995). *How to differentiate instruction in mixed-ability classrooms.* Alexandria, VA: Association for Supervision and Curriculum Development.

Tomlinson, C. A. (1999). *The differentiated classroom: Responding to the needs of all learners.* Alexandria, VA: Association for Supervision and Curriculum Development.

Tralli, R., Colombo, B., Deshler, D., & Schumaker, J. (1996). The strategies intervention model: A model for supported inclusion at the secondary level. *Remedial and Special Education, 17* (4), 204–216.

Udvari-Solner, A., & Thousand, J. (1996). Creating a responsive curriculum for inclusive schools. *Remedial and Special Education, 17* (3), 182–192.

Unsworth, L. (1984). Meeting individual needs through flexible within-class grouping of pupils. *The Reading Teacher, 38* (3), 298–304.

Vaughn, S., Bos, C. S., & Schumm, J. S. (2000). *Teaching exceptional, diverse, and at-risk students in the general education classroom* (2nd ed.). Boston: Allyn & Bacon.

Vaughn, S., Elbaum, B., & Schumm, J. (1996). The effects of inclusion on the social functioning of students with learning disabilities. *Journal of Learning Disabilities, 29* (6), 598–608.

Voeltz, L., Hemphill, N., Brown, S., Kishi, G., Klein, R., Fruehling, R., Collie, J., Levy, G., & Kube, C. (1983). *The special friends program: A trainer's manual for integrated school settings.* Honolulu: University of Hawaii, Department of Special Education.

Waldron, N., & McLeskey, J. (1998). The impact of a full-time inclusive school program (ISP) on the academic achievement of students with mild and severe learning disabilities. *Exceptional Children, 64* (2), 395–405.

Wang, M. (1987). Toward achieving educational excellence for all students: Program design and student outcomes. *Remedial and Special Education, 8* (3), 25–34.

Wang, M., & Birch, J. (1984). Comparison of a full-time mainstreaming program and a resource room approach. *Exceptional Children, 51* (1), 33–40.

Wasik, B., & Slavin, R. (1993). Preventing early reading failure with one-to-one tutoring: A review of five programs. *Reading Research Quarterly, 28* (2), 178–200.

Weller, D., & McLeskey, J. (in press). Block scheduling and inclusion in a high school: Teacher perceptions of the benefits and challenges. *Remedial and Special Education.*

Wesson, C., & Deno, S. (1989). An analysis of long-term instructional plans in reading for elementary resource room students. *Remedial and Special Education, 10* (1), 21–28.

Will, M. (1986). Educating children with learning problems: A shared responsibility. *Exceptional Children, 52* (5), 411–415.

Williamson, R. (1996). Middle level education. In J. Sikula, T. J. Buttery, & E. Guyton (Eds.), *Handbook of research on teacher education* (2nd ed.) (pp. 378–391). New York: Macmillan.

York, J., & Reynolds, M. (1996). Special education and inclusion. In J. Sikula, T. J. Buttery, & E. Guyton (Eds.), *Handbook of research on teacher education* (2nd ed.) (pp. 820–836). New York: Macmillan.

Zigmond, N. (1990). Rethinking secondary school programs for students with learning disabilities. *Focus on Exceptional Children, 23* (1), 1–22.

Zigmond, N., & Baker, J. (1997). A comprehensive examination of an experiment in full inclusion. In T. Scruggs & M. Mastropieri (Eds.), *Advances in learning and behavior disabilities: Volume 11* (pp. 101–134). Greenwich, CT: JAI Press.

Index

Please note that a page number followed by an *f* indicates a figure.

About the Authors

James McLeskey is professor and chair of the Department of Special Education at the University of Florida. Before moving to Florida in August 1999, he taught for 22 years at Indiana University. For the past 10 years, James has worked with many schools as they have attempted to develop and implement inclusive school programs. Through these endeavors, he has learned many lessons from teachers, principals, parents, and students regarding why it is important to develop inclusive programs and how these programs may be successfully developed. He has supplemented and enriched these lessons as a parent of two children who have had difficulty progressing in school.

Before working in higher education, James taught in the public schools in Anderson, South Carolina, as a teacher of students who were identified with learning disabilities, mild/moderate mental retardation, and emotional/behavioral disorders. He later worked in an early childhood model demonstration center for students with disabilities in Atlanta, Georgia.

James has published over 50 articles and chapters related to his work with students with disabilities, and has conducted over 200 workshops and conference presentations throughout the United States. He has also received several state and federal grants that addressed school reform and school improvement, preparing teachers to meet the needs of a diverse range of students in general education classrooms, and preparing leadership personnel in general and special education.

James can be contacted by e-mail at mcleskey@coe.ufl.edu or by mail at the Department of Special Education, University of Florida, G315 Norman Hall, P.O. Box 117050, Gainesville, FL 32611.

Nancy L. Waldron is an assistant professor in the Department of Educational Psychology at the University of Florida. She received her Ph.D. in school psychology from Indiana University (IU) in 1985 and was a research associate and assistant professor with the IU School Psychology Program before moving to Florida in 1999. Nancy has worked as a psychologist with a community mental health center and as a consultant to public schools, addressing topics such as the coordination of student support services, building-based intervention teams, and inclusive programs for students with disabilities.

Nancy has directed a series of state and federal grants that addressed the topics of inclusion and school change. These grants focused on achievement outcomes for general education students and students with disabilities in inclusive classrooms, training leadership personnel in school psychology, and providing professional development opportunities for teachers to develop inclusive school programs. Much of this work, along with her published articles and chapters, has focused on improving instructional and support services to accommodate a broad range of students with diverse needs in general education classrooms.

Nancy can be contacted by e-mail at waldron@coe.ufl.edu or by mail at the Department of Educational Psychology, University of Florida, 1412 Norman Hall, P.O. Box 117047, Gainesville, FL 32611.

Related Resources: Inclusion

ASCD stock numbers are noted in parentheses.

Audiotapes

Making Mainstreaming Work Through Prereferral Consultation: Myths and Possibilities by R. Evans (#61292036)

Print Products

Creating an Inclusive School, edited by Richard A. Villa and Jacqueline S. Thousand (#195210)

How to Untrack Your School by Paul George (#61192135)

Inclusion: A Fresh Look; Practical Strategies to Help All Students Succeed, Elementary Edition, by Linda Tilton (#398037)

The Inclusive School [Special issue]. *Educational Leadership,* v. 52, n. 4 (#1-94214)

Students with Special Needs [Special issue]. *Educational Leadership,* v. 53, n. 5 (#1-96006)

Videotapes

Inclusion (3 tapes) (#495044)

What's New in School—A Parent's Guide to Inclusion (#496221)

For additional resources, visit us on the World Wide Web (http://www.ascd.org), send an e-mail message to member@ascd.org, call the ASCD Service Center (1-800-933-ASCD or 703-578-9600, then press 2), send a fax to 703-575-5400, or write to Information Services, ASCD, 1703 N. Beauregard St., Alexandria, VA 22311-1714 USA.